# Great Lakes
# Serial
# Killers

### True Accounts of the Great Lakes
### Most Gruesome Murders

Wayne Louis Kadar

Avery Color Studios, Inc.
Gwinn, Michigan

© 2010 Avery Color Studios, Inc.

ISBN: 978-1-892384-56-0

Library of Congress Control Number: 2010903453

First Edition–2010

10   9   8   7   6   5   4   3   2   1

Published by Avery Color Studios, Inc.
Gwinn, Michigan 49841

# Table of Contents

This book is dedicated to the men and women of Law Enforcement; the Sheriff's Deputies, Police Officers, Constables, the Royal Canadian Mounted Police, the State Police and the Federal Agencies who put their lives on the line so the rest of us can sleep at night.

Thank you for all you do!

**Warning:** *This book is a collection of true stories of some of the most horrific crimes to occur in the Great Lakes Region. The text includes graphic descriptions of murder, rape, mutilation and sexual depravity.*

# Introduction

This book is not for children, those who are squeamish or those who are weak of heart. It is a compilation of true stories of some of the sickest minds to ever live in North America.

The collection includes men and women, who took pleasure in other's pain, people who killed others without remorse, and deviants who used others for their own perverse sexual gratification.

These individuals did not murder or practice their depraved acts on the waters of the Great Lakes, rather in the states and Canadian provinces making up the Great Lakes Region.

Each section is a recounting of the most shocking and bizarre crimes an individual or individuals perpetrated on others. The subjects of this book are real life mass murderers, serial killers and rapists.

# Only One Survived The Night Of Horror - Richard Speck

"Help me! Help me! All my friends are dead! Oh God, I am the only one alive!"

At 6:00 am on the morning of July 15, 1966, residents in the 2300 block of East 100th Street in Chicago, Illinois, woke up to the pitiful screams of a young woman. "Help me! Help me! All my friends are dead! Oh God, I am the only one alive!"

A Chicago police cruiser just happened to be passing by. Neighbors hearing the screams and ran to the street and stopped the cruiser. Officer Dan Kelly stopped. Seeing the girl standing on an outside ledge on the second floor of a townhouse, the officer assumed she was suicidal and threatening to jump. He called for assistance then went inside the townhouse to get to the girl.

As soon as he entered he made a grizzly discovery: the nude dead body of a young woman. He checked for a pulse, nothing and she was cold to the touch. He drew his pistol; this was no ordinary suicide case. He cautiously made his way up the stairs where he found another body. At the top of the stairs he looked in a bedroom, more bloody bodies.

By this time other police officers were arriving. Officer Kelly asked another officer to take the screaming girl down and out of the house while he made sure the killer was not still in the building.

Patrolman Kelly walked through the house, careful not to disturb any evidence the murderer might have left behind. In addition to the body he had found in the front room of the townhouse, at the top of the stairs the body of a young woman was laying half out of the bathroom. In a

front second floor bedroom three female corpses were lying on the floor and three more were in the next bedroom. Eight young women lay dead, brutally and viciously murdered.

The women were all student nurses enrolled in the South Chicago Hospital's nursing program. Five of the women were from Illinois or the surrounding states and three were exchange students from the Philippines.

The young woman who was screaming from the second floor, Corazon Amurao, an exchange student from the Philippines, was the only person in the house to survive. She was taken to the hospital, and although she was not harmed by the killer, she was suffering from the trauma of the ordeal and shock.

When she awoke, Miss Amurao told of the night of horror she and her roommates had endured and she gave a description of the man who did it.

The police were able to piece together the sequence of events from evidence found at the house and Miss Amurao's eyewitness account.

About 11:00 pm, an unknown man removed a window screen in the kitchen, reached in and unlocked the back door of the nurses' townhouse apartment. Once in, he crept around the apartment looking for something of value to steal. He stopped at a closed second floor door and knocked. Corazon Amurao answered the door to find a man standing in the doorway.

The white male in his mid twenties, about six feet tall with crew-cut hair, weighing about 170 pounds, flashing a butcher's knife in one hand and holding a small handgun in the other, pushed his way in the bedroom.

The man forced Miss Amurao to another bedroom, the middle bedroom on the second floor, where he awoke the three women sleeping in that room. The intruder made the four women go to the larger bedroom at the back of the second floor and woke up the two student nurses in that room.

The man told the girls that he wouldn't harm them; all he wanted was money to get to New Orleans. He used his knife to rip strips from sheets and bound the women's hands and legs. Then he demanded to know where their purses were.

Another student nurse who lived in the townhouse came in before the 12:30 am curfew. She was quickly moved into the back bedroom and made to lie on the floor with the others.

A short time later two other women, Susan Farris and Mary Ann Jordan came home. The man in the house surprised them in the upstairs hallway. They turned and ran, but the man sprinted after them. Angered by the women running from him, he chased them catching Miss Farris near the second floor bathroom. The man, his knife in hand, raised it and slammed it down, sinking the blade into Miss Farris's chest. In a fit of rage, he stabbed her eight more times in the chest and chin.

Mary Ann was caught in the front bedroom where she tried to hide. The knife, still dripping with Susan's blood, was thrust into Mary Ann multiple times. The killer stabbed her in the chest and neck and also viciously stabbed her in the left eye.

The murderer calmly washed his hands of the blood of the two women, then walked to the bedroom where the other women were tied up. He selected Pamela Wilkening as his next victim. He took her to the front bedroom where Mary Ann Jordan lay dead on the floor. The killer, without saying a word, buried the knife deep in her chest. Her wrists were still bound as the killer wrapped his fingers around her throat and choked the life out of the bleeding woman.

Nina Schmale was next. The murderer lifted the terrified girl to her feet and dragged her from the back bedroom. Nina shuffled along with him, her feet still tied together. She was taken to the left front bedroom, gagged and stabbed four times in the neck. The executioner, not content with the damage he inflicted on the poor girl, strangled her bleeding throat.

While the murderer was out of the room killing Nina Schmale, Corazon Amurao, slid under a bed and hugged the wall as tightly as possible. She remained there without making a sound as the rest of her friends were savagely killed.

The man returned to the room and dragged Valentina Pasion to her death. While her hands were still bound, she was strangled then he stabbed the student nurse several times. She was left on the floor of the front bedroom.

He next took another of the Philippine exchange students, Merlita Gargullo. The killer's rage seemed to become more intense. He dragged his knife along the neck of Miss Gargullo leaving a open gash. Her limp body fell to the floor and bled to death.

Patricia Matusek was pulled from the back bedroom. She was found in the front bedroom brutally beaten. An autopsy showed she was punched so hard that her liver had ruptured. Her cause of death was strangulation.

The murderer went back to the back bedroom for another victim. He jerked a terrified Gloria Davy to her feet. The girl, her hands bound behind her back with strips of bed sheets, was led down the stairs. Buttons bounced down the stairs as the murderer ripped Gloria's blouse from her body.

# Only One Survived The Night Of Horror

*Corazon Amurao, the sole survivor of the attack that took the lives of eight student nurses.*

Miss Davy was lead to the living room and forced to lay on the couch on her stomach. The killer jerked her pants and panties down and sodomized her. Then, or perhaps while he brutally raped her, he choked the breath out of her.

Content that he had killed all of the young women in the house and no one could identify him, the killer turned his attention to rummaging through their purses and stealing anything of value.

Corazon Amurao, hiding under the bed in the back bedroom, held her breath while the murderer went through the girls' belongings. She had not been missed or detected.

The man had left the back room where she was hiding but she could not be sure if the man had left the house. Corazon, terrified and afraid to move, remained hidden for several hours before she ran through the carnage to the front bedroom.

From Corazon Amurao's description the police artist made a sketch of the murderer. A clerk from the Maritime Union Hall notified the police that the drawing published in the newspapers resembled a man who had frequented the hall looking for work on the Great Lakes iron ore ships. His name was Richard Speck.

The police forensic team had found 32 bloody fingerprints in the nurse's house. The fingerprints were easily identified as belonging to an ex-con named Richard Speck.

Richard Speck had a lengthy record with the authorities. He had served jail time for theft, check forgery and aggravated assault. He was again arrested for assault and burglary in Texas, but he left the state before he was sentenced.

As the investigators delved into the background of their main suspect, they found that Speck was suspected in the murder and assault of other women.

He was wanted for questioning in the deaths of two Monmouth, Illinois, women; a barmaid who had refused his advances was found dead and five days later a 65-year-old woman was assaulted, raped and murdered.

Speck was also wanted in Indiana for questioning in the disappearance of three girls. The girls vanished during the same period of time that Speck was working on a Great Lakes freighter that was docked for repairs in an Indiana harbor.

Michigan authorities were also interested in Richard Speck. Four Benton Harbor, Michigan, females, ages 7, 19, 37 and 60 had been murdered. The freighter Speck was working on had been docked in Benton Harbor during the time of the murders.

The police knew who had committed the horrific murders of the eight student nurses. Now they had to find the criminal.

Five days after the deaths of the nurses, Richard Speck was captured. Whether he was consumed by guilt or just too egotistical to allow the police to catch him, Speck slashed his wrists in a suicide attempt.

In a change of heart after he had cut himself, he began to scream for help and an ambulance responded to his assistance. The emergency medical personnel provided immediate care for his wounds, then rushed him to the hospital. While treating the suicide patient, a doctor noticed

that this man resembled the police sketch of the man wanted in connection with the mass killings.

The doctor raised the man's shirtsleeve and found the "Born to Raise Hell" tattoo on his arm. The newspapers had written about the student nurse, Corazon Amurao, who had survived the savage attack. She described the killer as about six feet tall, about 170 pounds, crew cut hair and a tattoo on his forearm, which read, "Born to Raise Hell."

The doctor notified the police. Richard Speck was arrested for the death of the eight Chicago student nurses.

The trial of Richard Speck for the vicious murder of eight young women began on April 3, 1967. Expert witnesses testified of the 32 bloody fingerprints belonging to Speck found at the murder scene. Speck's confession was read to the jury. The police vividly described the horror of the crime scene. But, the most damning and most dramatic was when Cora Amurao, the only survivor of the women in the townhouse at 2319 E. 100th Street, pointed a finger directly at Speck and identified him as the man who, without remorse and in cold blood, had sadistically killed the eight student nurses.

The jury only took 49 minutes to decide the case and find Richard Speck guilty of eight counts of murder. They also recommended that Richard Speck be sentenced to die in the electric chair.

Due to a technicality in the legal system, Speck's death sentence was commuted to life in prison. He lived the remainder of his life in Statesville Prison in Crest Hill, Illinois.

The vicious murderer that so callously took the lives of eight young women, Richard Speck, died of a massive heart attack on December 5, 1991.

# The Murder At The Privacky Home - Seth Privacky

It was a warm Thanksgiving Day, November 29, 1998. At the Steven Privacky home at 1301 Riley – Thompson Road in Dalton Township, just outside Muskegon, Michigan, the family was preparing for the holiday dinner. Steven had gone to pick up his father John. Linda took a break from meal preparation to shower, Steven's oldest son Jedediah was watching TV, waiting for his girlfriend, April Boss, to arrive, and youngest son Seth was in his room.

Nineteen-year-old Jedediah Privacky was sitting in the family room at his parent's split-level home. Jed, as his family and friends called him, was a student enrolled in the Muskegon Community College's education program. His intentions were to remain at MCC one more year then transfer to Western Michigan University at Kalamazoo, Michigan, to complete his studies to become a teacher.

Jed and his longtime girlfriend, April Boss, were practically inseparable; both were 1997 graduates of Reeth – Puffer High School. She was attending MCC with Jed and, with her love of young children, she was a natural to also become a teacher. She and Jed had their plans all laid out. They would transfer to WMU and after graduation they would find teaching jobs and get married.

April Boss was always busy. To keep up with college expenses April worked the third shift at Grand Haven Plastics, and for enjoyment she sang in the choir at her church and spent as much time as she could with Jed. April was one of those special people to whom people gravitated. Her long red hair and her bubbly, engaging personality endeared her to others.

Linda Privacky, the mother of the household, had been working all morning on the family's Thanksgiving dinner. With the turkey in the oven, the salads in the refrigerator and the pie cooling on the counter, she went upstairs to take a shower.

Forty-nine years old Linda worked full time as an office assistant for an area neurologist, but her true love was gardening. Linda took pride in the fact she was a Master Gardener and past president of the West Michigan Herb Society. Each spring she enjoyed working at a local greenhouse assisting gardeners with selection of plants for planting.

A native of Charleston, South Carolina, Linda met her husband Steve while he was stationed there in the Navy. They fell in love, married and relocated to Steve's hometown.

Steve Privacky, a 50-year-old teacher in the Reeth – Puffer school district for 25 years, was well liked and respected by teachers and students alike. Steve had recently moved to the new intermediate school where he taught fifth grade and was very involved in school improvement committees and the school technology committee. On a district wide level, Steve worked with the local teacher's union on the contract negotiation team. He was instrumental in settling the last two contracts between the teachers union and the district.

Steve had picked up his father, John Privacky, for dinner. John, 78 years old, had recently had eye surgery and was not yet able to drive.

A retired linotype operator, John, whose wife had died five years earlier, was a handyman who enjoyed fixing things for his son and neighbors.

The family home had recently been purchased by Michigan's Adventure Amusement Park and the Privacky's were building a new house. Linda and Steve planned to move into their new White Lake Drive home after their youngest son, 18-year-old Seth, graduated from high school.

Seth was a senior in the Reeth – Puffer school district. He was a likeable teenager, polite and soft-spoken, but sort of a loner who hung out on the fringe. Some of his classmates considered Seth and his good friend, Steve Wallace, as "strange."

Unlike his older brother Jed, Seth had a penchant for getting in trouble. Nothing too bad, but a couple of shoplifting incidents caused a strain between Seth and his parents. The judge, who sat before Seth on the charge of theft of beer from a grocery store where Seth worked, ordered him and the family to attend counseling and for Seth to undergo psychological testing. Seth was later prescribed an antidepressant medication.

Seth argued with his parents, especially his father, quite regularly. Most arguments revolved around Seth's demands for freedom and what he perceived as his parent's overly strict rules.

Most recently the fights revolved around Seth buying his brother's car. He wanted the car but his parents would not approve because Seth's report card grades were not acceptable. Steve Privacky refused to loan Seth the money or co-sign for a loan, which angered Seth. So Seth asked his grandfather to co-sign for the loan. Grandpa John agreed, but when Seth's dad heard that Seth had gone behind his back, he was furious with Seth and put an end to the agreement. In turn, Seth was furious with his father. When brother Jed and Linda agreed with Steve, Seth was angry with them as well and accused them of ganging up on him.

On that warm November day in 1998, Seth's anger with his family boiled over. At 1:30 pm, Seth Privacky walked into the downstairs family room where his brother Jedediah was watching television. Seth raised a .22 caliber pistol and shot Jed in the back of the head. Blood and gray matter splattered the television set and nineteen-year-old Jed Privacky slumped down on the couch. He died instantly.

Seth heard his dad drive into the garage. Steve and Grandpa John had just arrived at the house. Seth walked into the garage and without saying a word, walked up to his father, pointed the gun at his father's head and pulled the trigger. The small caliber bullet penetrated Steve's skull and he fell dead to the floor.

Seth took aim at his grandfather and fired. The old man collapsed on the hard concrete floor. Seth heard his grandfather making gurgling noises as he attempted to breath, he wasn't dead. Seth took aim at his grandfather, the man who agreed to loan him the money to buy Jed's car, and shot him again.

Linda Privacky had not heard the shots because she was in the shower. Seth walked up the staircase to the bathroom and patiently waited until his mother stepped out of the shower.

Seth lifted the gun to within six inches of her forehead and fired a single shot. A small dark red spot appeared on her forehead as a shower of blood, skull and brains splattered the shower walls behind her. Linda's lifeless body fell on the cold tile floor of the bathroom, her blood pooling beneath her.

While upstairs, Seth heard a knock on the door. He went downstairs to find April Boss, Jed's girlfriend. April had let herself in. She had been invited to be part of the family Thanksgiving dinner as she had since the two had begun dating in high school. April was standing in the kitchen as Seth walked up to the unsuspecting girl, pointed the pistol at her from just a few feet away and shot her in the head.

Seth had completed the task he had been fantasizing about. He had killed his family; the family that had caused so much angst in his life. He was free of them.

Blood and death surrounded Seth; his brother in the lower level of the tri-level house with his head blown open by a gunshot, his mother was lying in a pool of blood on the upstairs bathroom floor, his father dead on the garage floor, his grandfather, who was shot twice, lay nearby and the beautiful and vivacious April Boss lay in a crumpled and bloody heap on the kitchen floor.

Seth called his friend Steve Wallace. Seth said frantically, "It's done; I did it."

At Seth's pleading Steve Wallace drove to the Privacky home. He found Seth outside the house, pacing, smoking a cigarette and crying. The full gravity of his actions had sunk in and Seth was an emotional wreck.

Seth sobbed as he told Wallace what he had done, how he had killed his family. Seth told Wallace not to go into the house, that it was too terrible.

Wallace was told that April Boss was killed because she walked in on the massacre and could identify Seth as the murderer, and Wallace was concerned that he might be killed next because he knew too much. Wallace asked Seth for the gun. He told him that he would dispose of the weapon; Seth handed it over.

Seth enlisted Wallace to help him drag the bodies of his family from the house, lift them into the car and take them somewhere for burial.

The two teens left a trail of blood as they dragged Steve Privacky's body from the garage to the driveway. When they tried to lift Steve's body into the car, they found that they couldn't lift the lifeless corpse. They needed a new plan.

The boys decided to make the scene look like a robbery.

Steve Wallace had errands he had to run. If he did not take care of them it might raise suspicions, so he left while Seth started cleaning and staging the robbery.

Steve Wallace first drove to Richards Park to throw the pistol and ammunition clip into the pond. Next he went to Blockbuster to return a video game. To avoid suspicion, Wallace continued with his evening's plans. He picked up a friend and they attended a church youth group meeting.

While Wallace was taking care of errands and trying to establish an alibi, Seth went to a Meier's discount department store. He threw the spent .22 caliber bullet casings in a trash can and purchased garbage bags and duct tape.

Sometime later in the evening, Seth picked up Wallace and the two returned to the Privacky house to arrange the bodies to look as through they were victims of a horrific robbery.

The Privacky house was set back from the road with the front yard filled with mature pine trees, providing coverage from the road and neighbors.

April Boss was scheduled to work the third shift that evening. When the normally extremely dependable employee did not show up for her shift, the company called her house.

Julie Boss Cooper, April's mother, and stepfather Tom Cooper drove to the Privacky house to see if April was still there and if she had forgotten about work.

April's parents arrived at the Privacky house just before midnight. As they drove into the driveway they saw that April's car was still there and their headlight shown on a shadowy figure leaning over what looked like a body in the driveway.

The safety of their daughter raced through her mind as Julie, at 11:58 pm, called 911.

"I am really worried because my daughter's car is here," she told the 911 operator.

She explained that when they drove up she saw a man in a plaid shirt bent over a bloody body.

The first police car arrived at 12:03 am. The Muskegon County Sheriff's department and the Michigan State Police surrounded the house. They suspected the killer was still in the house. But Seth and Steve Wallace had separately run into the woods before the authorities arrived.

The police captured Wallace as he came out of the woods. Seth avoided the police by running through the woods and across a golf course.

Seth found a place to sleep and awoke early in the morning when it started raining. In the rain, Seth hitchhiked along a country road.

An eighteen-year-old senior at Reeth-Puffer High School was driving on Webber road when she saw a hitchhiker standing on the side of the road.

She readily admits she is not one to pick up hitchhikers, but for some reason unknown to her, she took pity on the solitary figure standing in the rain and pulled over to pick him up.

As the hitchhiker opened the door of her car, she realized she had stopped for Seth Privacky.

She recognized him because they were classmates from school, and because the police had shown his photograph around school after he had killed his parents and April Boss. Authorities were worried he might show up at school. She knew he was wanted for murdering five people.

Seth climbed into the passenger seat of her car and thanked her for stopping. She realized she could not let on that she knew about the murders; she could not let on that she knew he was wanted by the police or she might be the sixth person Seth killed.

Seth and the terrified high school senior drove through the rain during the five-minute ride making small talk and the girl praying the Lord would take care of her. They arrived at a house on Duck Lake Road where a friend of Seth's lived. Seth thanked the girl for the ride and got out of the car.

When Seth got out and she drove away, the young lady began to shake uncontrollably and sobbed. She had just faced a murderer and lived

WEDNESDAY

**THE MUSKEGON Chronicle**

50 CENTS

DECEMBER 2, 1998 • 24 PAGES

# Son: I killed my family

Chilling details come to light in teen's confession

through it. She pulled out her cell phone but was so shaken she couldn't dial it. She pulled into the driveway of a nearby house. She ran screaming and crying to the house to use their phone to call the Sheriff's office.

Within minutes the deputies surrounded the house and the now passive Seth Privacky surrendered without a fight.

Under interrogation Seth told the investigators that he came home to find his brother Jedediah had flipped out and killed his girlfriend April, their father, mother and grandfather.

Seth told the authorities that Jed was irrational and begged Seth to kill him. Seth took pity on his brother and to end his brother's suffering, Seth took the gun and shot him in the head.

The Detective found the story very bizarre and continued to interrogate Seth until he broke down and admitted to shooting his family point blank, execution style, in the head. All except Grandpa John, who was shot twice in the neck.

The Muskegon County prosecutor, Tony Tague, brought Seth Privacky up on five counts of open murder. A Muskegon County jury found Seth guilty of all five counts and sentenced him to life in prison with no chance of parole. The 14th Circuit Court in Muskegon, Michigan, charged Steven Wallace with assisting Seth Privacky after Seth killed his family. He faced up to five years in prison but the jury acquitted him of the charges.

Seth is currently serving out a life sentence. Steve Wallace found his way into other troubles and later served a 28 month to 7½ year sentence in Muskegon County Jail.

## Great Lakes Serial Killers

A young man's momentary loss of control cost the lives of his father, his mother, his brother, his grandfather, and April. Now Seth Privacky lives incarcerated until he dies; he lives in his own hell, reliving how he killed his family on Thanksgiving Day in 1998.

# Detroit's Murderous Purple Gang

During the prohibition years, there were many individuals and several gangs that operated in the Detroit area. The close proximity of prohibition era Detroit to the rapidly flowing liquor of Canada made the area ripe for rum running. Some Detroit area gangs included the Oakland Sugar House Gang, The Third Street Gang and the most infamous of the gangs, the Purple Gang.

The Purple Gang began as a group of young Russian Jewish immigrant boys who had moved to the industrial city of Detroit with their parents and found that living in the land of milk and honey was not all it was advertised to be. Jobs, if they could be found, were low paying and the housing they could afford was usually in run-down neighborhoods; a breeding ground for thieves.

The four Bernstein brothers, Abe, Joe, Ray, and Izzy were the recognized leaders of the gang who began as vandals and shoplifters, stealing from shopkeepers and strong-arming other youths, but their criminal activities expanded to more violent crimes, as the boys grew older. It was said that they got their name from a shopkeeper after the thugs stole from his store. He said the youth were rotten; they were purple like rotten meat.

Robbery, breaking and entering, and extortion were soon crimes the gang excelled at but they would also strong-arm businessmen and rival gangs through the use of such methods as beatings, bombing, and murder.

When prohibition was enacted, the gang was quick to turn their attention to the money they could make selling liquor in the United States.

The Purple Gang found that there was more risk in smuggling the booze into the States than in selling it once it was in the States, so they made the distribution and sale their specialty. They purchased it from bootleggers, but more often they would hijack loads of liquor from individuals and other gangs. The Purples would not only steal the load of illegal alcohol but they would do it with Thompson machine guns blazing.

Because Detroit was so close to Canada, huge quantities of booze flowed across the river. It all wasn't consumed in Detroit, rather the booze was distributed all over the Midwest. Soon gangs from other cities looked at the profits that could be made by running rum across the Detroit River and they wanted a piece of the action. This led to bloody fights between the Purple Gang and other gangs.

By 1928, the Purple Gang had made millions of dollars in illegal activities but their own devices soon broke them up.

The Detroit Free Press headline of September 17, 1931 screamed of the murder of three gangsters. Like the St. Valentine's Day Massacre in Chicago, Detroit's criminals had brutally slaughtered three rival gang members.

Hymie Paul, Joe Sutker and Joe Lebowitz had last been seen alive at a club with Solly Levine and were said to be in high spirits when they left. The three men had been at odds with the Purple Gang for suspicion of

*Members of the notorious Purple Gang who violently ruled Detroit's prohibtion era illegal activities with an iron fist. From the Author's Collections.*

hijacking the Purple's trucks of booze, but the men were happy because Solly Levine had brokered a peace agreement and a meeting with the Purples.

Ray Bernstein, Irving Milburg, Harry Keywell and Harry Fleisher, all members of the Purple Gang, greeted the four men at the Collingwood Manor Apartments, apartment 211.

Levine, Paul and Lebowitz sat on the couch with Joe Sutker on the arm. Cigars were passed out and drinks poured. The conversation was light and Levine and the others relaxed. Bernstein made an excuse to leave and went to the car, started the engine and revved the engine loudly.

The loud engine was the signal for Irving Milburg, Harry Keywell and Harry Fleisher. When they heard it, the Purples pulled out their guns and began firing.

When the smoke cleared, Hymie Paul, Joe Sutker and Joe Lebowitz lay in a large pool of coagulating blood, all three were still holding their cigars. Solly Levine stood looking at the bodies, waiting for one of the mobsters to turn towards him and take aim, but rather they asked if he was ok.

A witness said she watched out her kitchen window disgusted with a car near the back of the apartments revving its engine and causing it to backfire several times. As she watched, four men ran from the apartment, jumped into the car and the vehicle sped away screeching its tires on the pavement.

The killers had planned the assassination of the mobsters in advance. The .38 Colt pistols used had their serial numbers filed off and the mobsters had taken a bucket of green paint and placed it in the kitchen. After they had gunned down Sutker, Paul and Lebowitz, the murderers tossed the pistols into the bucket of paint so finger prints could not be detected.

The three killers and Solly Levine sped off. Solly was waiting for one of them to put a hole in his head. Later it came to light that Ray Bernstein had plans for Levine. The plan was to later kill Levine and plant evidence on him indicating he was the killer of Sutker, Paul and Lebowitz.

The three dead men were no choirboys caught in a gangland crossfire. Hymie Paul, Joe Sutker and Joe Lebowitz were brought to Detroit originally as enforcers for the Oakland Sugar House Gang to strong arm legitimate businessmen, and collect from rumrunners. They soon tired of doing the work and not getting a large enough part of the profits. They fell out of favor with the other Detroit gangs partly because of their repeatedly hijacking rival loads of whiskey, encroaching on other gangs' territory and killing at random. They were unpredictable, they held allegiance to no one. Their deaths were heralded by the Detroit underworld as a good thing, but not by the public.

The brutal murders outraged the citizens of Detroit and prosecuting attorney Harry S. Toy. An all out manhunt was mounted to find the men responsible for maliciously killing the three gangsters. Tips were phoned into the police, probably from rival gangs taking advantage of the opportunity to get rid of the Purples.

Their warring with other gangs resulted in bloody battles with bodies piling up until the public would no longer stand for it. The Detroit newspapers screamed for the violence to stop and for witnesses to step forward to break the hold the gang held on Detroit. Investigators were able to tie several crimes to Purple Gang members, sending many key members to prison and the effectiveness of the gang was soon diminished.

# The Murdering Meat Packer Of Chicago - Adolph Luetgert

Adolph Luetgert was an imposing figure. He was a large burly man with a full head of hair and a thick mustache. He immigrated to Chicago from Germany in the early 1870s with his wife and two children. In his homeland he had learned the craft of making fine German sausage.

Luetgert's sausage was enjoyed by family and friends and soon he began making and selling his specialty in Chicago. Through determination and hard work, Adolph's sausage was soon in demand and his business grew. By 1894, Mr. Luetgert had built a five-story building on the corner of Hermitage and Diversey Parkway to house his meatpacking business.

He also built a three-story frame house next to the sausage plant for his wife and children. The family was waited on by a staff of servants willing to satisfy their every whim.

Adolph was absorbed by his business, and his wife was left to tend to the house and children until she became sick. She lingered in a sickly state for a while until she succumbed to her illness.

Mr. Luetgert was not a man to sit around and mourn the passing of his wife. In just two months following his wife's death, Adolph married Louise Bricknee.

Louise and Adolph were immediately smitten with one another. The large rotund man was taken with the small waif-like woman who looked more like a girl than a woman.

Louise was in turn fascinated with the man of wealth who courted her, despite the fact that she was more than ten years younger than the

man. His loud boisterous demeanor seemed to compliment her shy retiring personality. Louise was also impressed that Mr. Luetgert had servants in his house, since that was what she was, a servant for another family.

To show his love for his new petite young bride, the meat packer had a gold wedding ring made. The ring had Louise's married initials engraved inside the band; "L.L.".

Three children were born to the couple and Louise stayed home and cared for all five children and managed the household while Adolph, it is said, ran around with other women. He was often seen entertaining women at the sausage plant after business hours.

The couple's happy marriage turned sour, they argued frequently. Their disagreements were the talk of the neighborhood. Finally fed up with his nagging wife, Luetgert moved from the house to a small room in the meatpacking plant.

At one time Mr. Luetgert went to the police to report that he thought his wife was seeing a secret lover behind his back. The police were aware of the reputation of Mr. Luetgert as a womanizer and ignored his complaint.

On May 1, 1897, Louise went to visit her sister and decided to stay with her, at least that is what Adolph told the children to explain her absence from the home. He told others that Louise had left him for another man with whom she had been having a torrid love affair, leaving him to care for the five children.

Several days after Louise went missing and not being able to contact her, Louise's brother, Dietrich Bricknee, went to the police.

The case was assigned to Detective Herman Schuetter. During his initial investigation, the hard-nosed investigator spoke with the neighbors of the Luetgert family.

The detective was told of the loud and sometimes-violent arguments heard coming from the house.

He also interrogated employees of the sausage plant. One worker at the plant told the police that Mr. Luetgert often had women visit him at the plant after he thought everyone had left.

The most recent and frequent visitor was Mary Simerling. Mary was a servant and the niece of Adolph's wife, Louise,

The Chicago Police suspected that possibly Louise Luetgert did not leave the meatpacking plant of her own will; maybe her domineering husband had done away with the frail young woman, the mother to his five children.

Rumors ran rampant through the neighborhood and beyond. Had the sausage king killed his wife? Had the sausage maker added Louise to his secret recipe?

Sales of Luetgert plummeted. No one wanted to feed Louise to their family!

A worker told the police that he had seen both Mr. and Mrs. Luetgert at the sausage plant about 10:30 pm, the evening before Mrs. Luetgert vanished. The night watchman confirmed seeing them as well. The watchman remembered it because Mr. Luetgert sent him on an errand and then sent him home early.

Detective Schuetter realized that the meatpacking plant had been closed for several weeks prior to Louise's disappearance for cleaning and reorganizing. Yet despite being

ADOLPH LUETGERT.

closed the day before Louise vanished, Mr. Luetgert placed an order for 378 pounds of potash and 50 pounds of acid.

This led the detective to suspect that maybe Mrs. Luetgert had not been ground into sausage filler as so many thought, but rather Adolph had disposed of his wife like he disposed of waste animal parts in his sausage plant.

Wastes that could not be used in making sausage, like heads, hooves, blood, bone and viscera were put in a rendering vat, soaked with acid until the meat became liquid and the smaller bones melted. Any solid material left after the acid baths were burned in the stove with the caustic potash.

The police searched the entire five-story meatpacking plant for clues that Louise had met with foul play and died at the hand of her husband.

They found in a twelve foot long and five foot deep rendering vat workers used to melt the flesh of the animal waste parts, a small fragment of bone. Other officers noticed that a congealed mass was on the floor near the vat. It had apparently sloshed out of the vat. With sticks the police combed through the rancid substance finding several small pieces of bone.

George A. Dorsey, a Physical Anthropologist at Chicago's Field Museum of Natural History, was called on to see if he could determine whether the bones found in the vat and in the congealed puddle of fat on the floor were animal or human.

Mr. Dorsey identified the bone found in the fat to be a small fragment of a human skull. The other bones recovered from the putrid pile on the floor were found to be a human finger bone, part of a human toe bone, a small piece of a human rib bone, and a small piece of bone from the foot of a human.

The final object the Chicago Police found in the mass of melted fat on the meatpacking plant floor was a gold wedding ring. The initials "L.L." were engraved inside the gold band.

Adolph Luetgert, the man who made a fortune selling fine quality German sausage, was arrested for the murder of his second wife, Louise.

Mr. Luetgert was brought before a judge and jury on the charge of murdering his wife and explained that he had kept the ring in his breast pocket since his wife had left, saying he was comforted by keeping the ring near his heart, for he knew his beloved wife would soon return. He theorized the ring must have fallen from his pocket as he went about his

## 𝕸𝖚𝖗𝖉𝖊𝖗𝖊𝖗'𝖘 𝕱𝖆𝖙𝖆𝖑 𝕸𝖎𝖘𝖙𝖆𝖐𝖊

**HAD ADOLPH LUETEGERT REMOVED RINGS FROM WIFE'S FING-
ERS HE MIGHT HAVE ESCAPED CONVICTION, SAYS SLEUTH,**

(Chicago Tribune )

RS LOUISE L. LUETGERT, the second wife of Adolph L. Luetgert, disappeared from her home at Hermitage avenue and Diversey boulevard on the night of May 1, 1807. This disappearance furnished Chicago with one of the greatest mysteries in its history.

regaling the sausage maker just prior to the arrest were unanswerable "Not long ago," said Captain Schuettler, "you made a vigorous appeal to me to find a dog that belonged to you. Not you did not report the absence of your wife."

Adolph Luetgert's domestic life was not

normal duties at the plant. But he could not explain how human bones came to be found in the rendering vat or in the mess on the floor.

Mr. Dorsey told the court that the bones found at the sausage plant were of human origin. This was the first time a scientist testified before a judge and jury making it the first case in history that scientific forensic evidence was presented in court.

The jury could not rationalize convicting a man when there was no dead body found. How could they send a man to jail for the rest of his life when his wife might have just run away? The trial ended with a hung jury.

The prosecution team felt so confident with the evidence they presented that they re-tried the case. The second jury, in 1898, found the meat packer guilty of murdering his wife Louise, the mother of his five children.

Adolph Luetgert, the German immigrant sausage maker, was sentenced to life in prison. He was sent to the correctional facility in Joliet, Illinois.

Prison guards told of how Adolph was haunted by the ghost of Louise. He would cry out at night in his jail cell as she haunted him for killing her, mutilating her body and denying her a proper burial.

On July 30, 1899, Adolph Luetgert, the murdering meat packer died.

The Luetgert house was rented out for a while but the tenants kept complaining that the spirit of Louise haunted the home. They claimed the ghostly image of Louise, dressed in a white flowing gown, was often seen leaning against the fireplace. Renters never lived in the house for long.

Today, the Luetgert house has been torn down but the five-story sausage plant has been converted to condominiums. One can only wonder if Louise Bricknee Luetgert still visits what was once the rendering room.

# Detroit's Most Prolific Serial Killer - Shelly Brooks

In August of 2001, Sandra Davis, a poor black woman, was killed on the east side of Detroit. No one noticed. The 53-year-old woman was on the streets turning tricks to support her addiction to crack cocaine.

The addiction maintained such a strangle hold on her that nothing was more important than where and when she would find her next "bump".

No one noticed her missing. Anyone who might miss her, family and friends, were a part of her previous life. The morals she had learned from her grandmother were long forgotten. Her family, unable to help with her addiction, had long ago given up on her. Sandra Davis was not missed.

The man who killed her had raised a concrete block above her, smashed it down on her head and left her lifeless, bloody, naked body in an abandoned house. Her body lay on the floor for weeks before her decomposing corpse was discovered.

Her death was investigated by the Detroit Police Department but there was very little evidence. Nobody saw her with anyone prior to her death; no one saw her enter the building. No one noticed she was missing.

In February of 2002, a police officer on the night shift was patrolling on Detroit's east side when a screaming woman flagged him down. The homeless woman had entered an abandoned apartment building looking for a place to sleep. It was the same building where six months earlier the body of Sandra Davis was found.

The homeless lady noticed a pile of carpet in the corner of one of the rooms. Thinking it would be more comfortable than the hard wood floor,

# Great Lakes Serial Killers

she lifted the carpet and found the bloody body of another woman. She screamed in horror and ran from the building.

The police cautiously entered the building, weapons drawn and the beams of their flashlights illuminating the darkness. They searched the building room by room but they didn't find anyone in the building, just the body of the woman.

The nude woman was on her back with her legs spread open. Her head had been repeatedly struck with a heavy object. Her fingerprints later identified her as Pamela Greer, 33 years old, a local woman with a history of prostitution and drug abuse.

The autopsy revealed she had unprotected sex just prior to her murder. Forensics took a swab of her vagina for DNA analysis.

Between the years of 2001 and 2006, five more bodies of east side prostitutes were discovered.

The Detroit Police noted the similarities of the murders. They were all found in abandoned buildings and vacant lots. They were all severely bludgeoned with a heavy objects: a concrete block, a brick, a table leg or a board. Each victim was nude and posed after death in the same spread eagle fashion. The victims were then covered with something: pieces of clothing, an old blanket or discarded pieces of carpet.

The police were looking for a person or persons who were now classified as serial killers.

Mike Carlisle was assigned to be the lead investigator on the case. Carlisle, a detective with the homicide division, had been with the Detroit Police Department for 21 years and was considered one of the finest homicide detectives.

Detective Carlisle didn't care how the victims lived their lives; they might be prostitutes or dope dealers, he did his best to bring their murderer to justice.

Over the five-year period since the first decomposed body was discovered, bodies of women were being found at an alarming rate. The women were Sandra Davis, 53, Pamela Greer, 33, Marion Woods-Daniels, 36, Rhonda Myles, 45, Thelma Johnson, 30, Melissa Toston, 38, and a seventh victim whose body was too decomposed to be identified. They were mothers, daughters, wives, and sisters who lived a tragic life and met a violent end.

In the murders of the seven women, Detective Carlisle had little evidence with which to work. The victims were all drug-addicted prostitutes who had lost contact with or been cast out from their families. Their lifestyles were such that disappearing for days on end was not unusual. It was also not unusual that no one noticed the victims were missing until their body was discovered.

The file folders stacked up on Detective Carlisle's desk. But, there was little evidence for him to pursue until in June, 2006, a woman, Marsha May, 45, was found running naked and screaming from an abandoned building. Blood was running down her face from the savage beating she had endured.

Detroit Police and emergency medical personnel quickly responded. The woman was taken to the hospital where she slipped into a coma. This was the break the police were waiting for, a victim who had survived an attack from the serial killer.

When the woman regained consciousness, she was able to describe to police the man who severely beat her. He was a man she had seen around the neighborhood but she knew only as "E." She described him as tall; very tall.

Marsha May told police that she went with the man to an abandoned building, had sex with him and then smoked some crack. Then they went to another building to smoke some more crack but rather he violently and sexually assaulted her and then beat her head with a brick, and left her for dead.

*Shelly Brooks in a booking photograph.*

The police identified the man nicknamed "E" as Shelly Brooks. Brooks was named as a person of interest in the attack on Marsha May and possibly in the murder of seven other women.

Standing six foot four inches tall, Shelly Brooks was a 38-year-old man who grew up on Detroit's east side called the Cass corridor. His description was given to all patrol cars. Police officers questioned street people and their informants as to the whereabouts of "E".

One of the informants came through with information that the man they were searching for had been seen entering an abandoned building. The Detroit Police went to the building where Shelly Brooks was taken into custody without resistance.

Shelly Brooks was a drifter who worked at various jobs and throughout the years was often homeless, existing by sleeping in the abandoned buildings so prevalent throughout Detroit's east side, and eating at churches and food kitchens.

A DNA sample taken from Brooks was analyzed and found to match the sample taken from one of the dead women, Pamela Greer. During interrogation Brooks admitted to killing the seven prostitutes. He said he blamed prostitutes and drug dealers for the condition of the city.

In addition to the seven dead prostitutes whose corpses were found with similar characteristics, seven additional female bodies had been found. Many of the other dead women shared some characteristics of the seven women Shelly Brooks admitted to killing, but the similarities were not enough for Detroit Police to quantitatively state they were killed by the same person. Shelly Brooks was not formally accused nor did he admit to killing these women.

When word hit the streets that Shelly Brooks was arrested for the murder of the prostitutes, many who knew him were surprised. Shelly Brooks was known as an articulate and polite man. Others referred to Brooks as a loner and didn't think the Shelly Brooks they knew was capable of such heinous crimes.

Shelly Andre Brooks claimed that he had sex with the women but did not kill them and that he made a confession only after the Detroit Police had beaten him. Despite his proclamation of innocence, Brooks was sentenced to life in prison for the death of one woman. Just eight days later Brooks was found guilty in the beating death of another woman and was sentenced to an additional 25 to 50 years.

Shelly Brooks, the six-foot four inch polite loner has gone into the record books as the most prolific serial killer in Detroit's history.

# Wisconsin's Original Serial Killer - Eddie Gein

Small rural towns are not protected from the wrath of a serial killer. One of the most infamous of killers committed his crimes in a small Wisconsin town. His name has become synonymous with mass death and bizarre mutilation of dead bodies. His exploits have inspired books and movies. He is Edward Gein.

Edward Theodore Gein was born on August 27, 1906 and lived his first eight years in La Crosse, Wisconsin, with his father, mother and older brother.

La Crosse, Wisconsin, is located on the western border of Wisconsin along the Mississippi River. In 1906, La Crosse was a tough river town where steamboats loaded passengers, cattle and crops grown in the area and shipped them down the Mississippi to the large river towns to the south.

About this time was also the era of the lumber boom. Loggers went north and worked all winter clearing the vast stretches of virgin growth white pine, then they followed the logs south along the Mississippi and its tributaries to the mills and ports where the lumber was shipped out to the growing cities to the south. La Crosse was a natural port town that attracted the hard working and hard drinking lumber and river men. As with most boom towns, where the men went the saloons and prostitutes followed.

Eddie's mother, Augusta Gein, was a strict parent dedicated to shielding her boys, Eddie and his older brother, Henry, from the immorality of the world. To save the boys from a life of hell and

damnation, she schooled them to strictly obey the Word of the Lord and beat into them the dangers of loose women.

The father of the two boys, George Gein, was not a strong man and did not have a say in the raising of the children. He allowed Augusta to raise their boys to be God fearing, righteous young men.

The family moved from La Crosse and its evil ways to the rural farming community of Plainfield, Wisconsin.

Augusta thought the 195-acre farm the family purchased in 1914 was far enough removed from society that Henry and Eddie would not be seduced by the devil's ways so prevalent in the larger cities. The evils of the world would be kept at a distance and Augusta could raise her boys according to her strict, fanatical religious beliefs.

Although, despite her desire to keep the boys pure and untouched from the outside world, the boys would have to eventually attend school.

Henry and Eddie did not excel academically and were understandably somewhat socially maladjusted. They did not develop any strong friendships; in fact, they had no friends at all.

After the boy's father, George Gein died, the two boys would do anything to earn money to supplement the family income. The two boys were known in Plainfield for the odd jobs and handyman work they did for neighbors and around the area. Eddie especially enjoyed babysitting.

As the boys grew older, Henry began to rebel against his mother's tyrannical domineering ways. He began to question her and criticize her about her religious beliefs and thoughts on immorality. Eddie blindly followed and never doubted his mother. A rift began to develop between the brothers, which might have ultimately resulted in Henry's mysterious death in 1944.

A grass fire was burning near the Gein farm and, fearing it would spread to their farm, Augusta sent the boys to put it out. Henry and Eddie separated and attacked the flames from different directions. As it grew darker, Eddie realized he could no longer see his brother so he went looking for Henry. Not able to locate Henry and fearing he may have been overcome by smoke, Eddie contacted the police for help. The police found Henry lying dead on the ground.

The police had suspicions that the death was not accidental, facts like Henry's body was laying on a section of ground that had not been burned. Most of the area had been burned except that small area where Henry was found. Something else the police found odd was that Eddie claimed he could not find Henry but when they arrived on the scene, Eddie led them right to the body.

But what really raised the suspicions of the police was that there were unexplained bruises on the back of Henry's head.

Despite their suspicions, the police could not believe that the shy, quiet Eddie could have anything to do with his brother's death. The coroner determined the cause of death to be asphyxiation as a result of smoke inhalation.

Henry was dead so he could no longer question his mother's tyrannical domination. It was now just Eddie and his mother.

*The gentle mass murderer of Wisconsin, Eddie Gein. From the Author's Collection.*

On December 29, 1945, Eddie's world collapsed when Augusta Gein, the most important person in his life, died of a stroke.

Eddie remained on the farm and earned subsistence living off the babysitting and handyman jobs he found. The rooms of the farmhouse where Augusta spent the most time were boarded off and they remained just as they were when she was alive. Eddie created a shrine to his mother.

Outwardly, Eddie seemed to be handling the death of his mother okay, but the little strange man was becoming stranger, even bizarre. Free from his mother's iron fisted rule, Eddie engaged in satisfying some of the guilty pleasures his mother lectured him about.

Eddie was always an avid reader and adventure books provided him an escape from the reality of his world. But after Augusta's death, his taste in literature changed. He began reading books and magazines about death cults, Nazi's, and was especially intrigued with tales of shipwrecked sailors on remote South Pacific islands; islands where the sailors who had the misfortune to land were killed and cannibalized. Eddie also sought out instructions on how the South Pacific natives shrunk the heads of their enemies.

Quiet, reclusive, effeminate, Eddie Gein's behavior was changing radically. His mind was in turmoil; he desired everything his mother had taught him was evil. The full depths of his depravity would soon become apparent as people around Plainfield, Wisconsin, began to go missing.

The police were worried that the mysterious disappearances might be connected, although there were no connections between the four that the police were able to determine. The first was an eight-year-old girl who

disappeared while walking home from school. Next a fifteen-year-old girl went missing while she was babysitting. A few years later, two hunters stopped in Plainfield and were never seen again. A Plainfield tavern owner, Mary Hogan, was next to vanish; all that remained was a trail of blood on the tavern floor leading to the parking lot.

On November 16, 1957, 58-year-old Bernice Worden disappeared from the hardware store she owned and operated. Her son, Frank Worden, a Deputy Sheriff, returned from deer hunting and stopped by the store. He was concerned because his mother was nowhere to be found. He called the Sheriff and began to look around. He grew very concerned for his mother's well-being when he found a trail of blood leading to the back door.

The police arrived and started their investigation into the disappearance of Mrs. Worden. They discovered something that was not incriminating but might help in their investigation. The last sales receipt was written out for anti-freeze. Frank Worden remembered that Eddie Gein said he would come into town that morning for anti-freeze.

That evening law enforcement authorities went to the Gein farm to question Eddie. He wasn't necessarily a suspect but it was apparent that he was at the hardware store and made the last purchase before Mrs. Worden disappeared.

Sheriff Arthur Schley walked through Eddie Gein's dark kitchen, illuminated only by the flashlight the Sheriff carried. The room was cluttered with garbage and stunk of rotting food. As the Sheriff looked around the kitchen, he felt something brush against his jacket. When his flashlight shown on the object he brushed against, he found a sight that would cause a lesser man to vomit. It was the headless body of a woman hanging from the ceiling beams. The body had been slit open and gutted like a deer and hung over the sink for the blood to drain from the carcass.

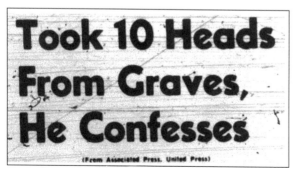

**Took 10 Heads From Graves, He Confesses**

(From Associated Press, United Press)

Eddie Gein was taken into custody and a complete search of the premises

# Confesses to Slayings
# of At Least 2 Women

## Townsfolk Ask Queries on Skulls

(From Associated Press, United Press)

WAUTOMA — Edward Gein confessed he killed at least two women.

The 51-year-old bachelor farmer who admitted during two days of questioning at the State Crime Laboratory at Madison that he killed two women and looted graves for the cadavers of at least nine more, faces a murder arraignment and sanity hearing "as soon as possible."

### Charge Today

Waushara County District Atty. Earl Kileen said Wednesday afternoon that he would file the murder charge against Gein today if the crime lab's ballistics report was ready by then.

"I will move immediately for a sanity hearing when he is arraigned," the prosecutor said.

This count will charge Gein with the shooting and subsequent mutilation of Mrs. Bernice

began. What the Sheriff's Department found was overwhelming even by today's standards. It was a house of horrors.

The inventory at the house included ghoulish objects one would only expect to find in a low budget horror movie. Lampshades and wastebaskets were made of human flesh, tanned and stretched taut over a frame. A bowl found in the kitchen that showed signs of use was made from the top of a human skull and preserved shrunken heads were found hanging on a wall as decorations.

A shoe box found in Eddie Gein's bedroom contained souvenirs of Eddie Gein's exploits, dried female genitalia. Other items found were a preserved human head, four noses cut from their victims faces, a pair of lips on a string, nine death masks, skulls adorning his bedposts, a heart removed from a corpse and a belt Eddie adorned with nipples from the breasts of the women he killed or corpses he mutilated.

The most bizarre of Eddie Gein's collection was later found. It was an object that would inspire the movie "Silence of the Lambs" and Alfred Hitchcock's "Psycho." The investigators found a suit Eddie had fashioned of human flesh. He selected parts of the bodies of the women he killed or dug up, dried the flesh, then pieced together the full body suit of a female. The suit was complete with female breasts.

During the first day of interrogation by the Wautoma County Sheriff's Department, Eddie Gein refused to talk. But the next day he began to talk to the authorities about how he killed Mrs. Worden. He claimed he was in a dazed state and couldn't remember all of the details but what he confessed to was dragging her body out of the hardware store to his Ford, driving her back to the farm where he shot her in the head with a .22 caliber gun.

The mild mannered Eddie Gein told the officers that most of the body parts found at the house he had taken from graves. Eddie would visit the cemetery and dig up the graves of freshly buried women. He adamantly swore that he had not killed anyone else; that all of the body parts he pilfered from graves.

Under further interrogation, Eddie admitted to killing Mary Hogan at the tavern. As with the killing of Mrs. Worden, Gein said he didn't remember any of the details of the Mary Hogan killing because of his dazed state.

The search continued at the Gein farm where more body parts were found. The authorities resolved that the only way they would know for sure if the body parts were from graves or from females Gein murdered was to exhume the graves. While many of the graves showed signs of

**Wisconsin ▲ State Journal**

SECTION 1 · MORNING FINAL · MADISON, TUESDAY, NOVEMBER 19, 1957 · ★ ★ ★ · 5c

# STATE FARMER SAYS HE KILLED WHILE IN DAZE

## Took 10 Heads From Graves, He Confesses

tampering, not all of the body parts found on the Gein farm could be verified to have come from graves.

Eddie Gein underwent several psychological evaluations to determine his mental state. The psychiatrists determined that Eddie was indeed mentally impaired. He was ordered to be housed in the Central State Hospital for the Criminally Insane at Waupun, Wisconsin, until he could be determined sane enough to stand trial.

After ten years in the mental institution, in 1968, Eddie Gein was deemed competent to stand trial for the murder of Bernice Worden. After a week of testimony, Eddie Gein was found guilty of murder but deemed insane when he committed the crime. The conviction was thrown out and he was sent back to the institution of the criminally insane and moved to the Mendota Mental Health Institute at Madison, Wisconsin, in 1978.

**Wisconsin ▲ State Journal**

SECTION 1 · MORNING FINAL · MADISON, THURSDAY, NOVEMBER 21, 1957 · ★ ★ ★ · 5c

Confessor's Victims

# GEIN FACES MURDER CHARGE, SANITY TEST

Funeral Services Held for Mrs. Worden

## Confesses to Slayings of At Least 2 Women

Edward Theodore Gein remained there until July 26, 1984 when he died after a long battle with cancer. He was buried in Plainfield, Wisconsin, next to his mother and surrounded by the graves he plundered.

The bizarre life and exploits of Edward Gein spawned books and movies. He was the basis of the characters Norman Bates in Alfred Hitchcock's "Psycho" and Buffalo Bill from the movie "Silence of the Lambs." Some concepts of the Eddie Gein saga were incorporated into other stories and movies as well.

Edward Gein was the worst serial killer in the annals of Wisconsin's history. He didn't kill many but he killed and mutilated the bodies and kept ghoulish souvenirs of his victims. He was Wisconsin's worst serial killer until the Milwaukee police discovered the apartment of Jeffery Dahmer.

# Michigan's Coed Murderer - John Norman Collins

The cities of Ypsilanti and Ann Arbor, Michigan are separated by just over seven miles geographically, but in reality they are worlds apart. Ypsilanti is a blue-collar industrial city while Ann Arbor is a city whose tax base leans more towards research and technological innovative companies.

Eastern Michigan University in Ypsilanti is well known for its school of education and Ann Arbor is closely tied to the multicultural University of Michigan. Ypsilanti has been known for its large population of families who relocated from the southern states for employment in Michigan's once lucrative automobile industry. Ann Arbor's population has more of an international composition, with the university attracting educated people with diverse cultural backgrounds.

Yet Ypsilanti and Ann Arbor were brought together when the dead, mutilated, nude bodies of young women began appearing in and around the two communities.

On August 7, 1967, three teenagers working on a farm heard the slam of a car door and went to check it out.

By the time they arrived where they thought the sound came from there weren't any cars in the area but there looked to be a path freshly made as though someone had been driving through the grass and woods. The boys followed the path and they began to smell a putrid odor like that of a decomposing dead deer. A few feet further they made a horrifying discovery; something rotting that looked like a dead body.

At first the boys suspected it was the body of an animal, the torso was black and gray, resembled leather and was covered with flies and

maggots. When one of the boys saw the rancid corpse had what looked to be a human ear, they realized that they had stumbled upon a human body. The boys notified the Michigan State Police.

The Ypsilanti Medical Examiner was given the task of determining the identity of the body. The work was complicated by the fact that the person had been dead for over a month and the body was badly decomposed; it was not even obvious if the body was a male or female. Also, fingerprints could not be used since one arm was cut off below the elbow and the fingers were sliced off from the fingers of the other hand. The body had been further mutilated by the perpetrator, who had cut off both of the victim's feet.

The Medical Examiner was able to identify the corpse through dental records. The decaying body was that of 19-year-old Mary Fleszar. The coroner determined that before death she had been severely beaten then savagely stabbed in the chest about thirty times.

Ms. Fleszar, an accounting major at Eastern Michigan University, was last seen on the evening of July 9, 1967. She had told her roommate she was going out for a walk and mysteriously never came back.

A team of Michigan State Police investigators swarmed over the scene. They discovered among the debris strewn about in the area a sandal and an orange dress printed with white dots which was identified as the clothing Mary Fleszar was last seen wearing.

The investigators were able to determine that Mary had been killed at another location and dumped at the farm. Evidence also indicated that the body had been moved at least four times since it had been placed at the farm site. Had the killer or killers revisited the rotting corpse and rearranged it?

The police interviewed people living in Mary Fleszar's neighborhood to inquire if they had seen Mary that evening. Several had seen her walking but nothing seemed out of the ordinary. But one man who knew Mary reported seeing her walking on the sidewalk when a bluish-gray Chevrolet stopped to talk to her. He saw her shake her head no, and then the car drove on.

The man observed the same car drive by once more and again stopped by Ms. Fleszar. He watched Mary for a second time shake her head no to the man driving the car. The apparently frustrated driver screeched his tires as he sped off down the street.

Another body was discovered just two days shy of a year of the date Mary Fleszar left her apartment. Workmen at a construction site discovered the body of a young woman.

The victim was found nude except for her miniskirt that was twisted around her neck. Her skin was blackened due to decomposition, her throat had a large gapping hole where it had been slashed and she had been stabbed at least five times in the chest.

The body was identified as Joan Schell. Joan, an art major at Eastern Michigan University, was hitchhiking the night of June 30, 1968, when she was observed getting into a car with three young men who offered her a ride.

Five days later she was found dead.

A friend of Joan's told the police that Joan had dated a guy who lived across the street from Joan's apartment. An investigator interviewed the 23-year-old man. He told police he never dated the girl and didn't even know her. The man was clean cut, well spoken and convincing. The man, John Norman Collins, was not considered a suspect.

A twenty-three years old University of Michigan law student, Jane Mixter, was looking for a ride to Muskegon, Michigan, to visit her parents. She called them saying she had found a ride with a guy named David Johnson. He was driving there on March 20, 1968, and offered to take her along.

The following day her body was found in a Denton Township cemetery. She had been strangled and shot in the head two times with a

.22-caliber pistol. Her skirt was up around her waist and her pantyhose pulled down around her knees, yet she had not been sexually assaulted. A yellow raincoat covered her body. Like the others, Jane had been killed at a different location and dumped at the cemetery.

Investigators checked out all David Johnson's who lived in the area or had any connection with either of the universities. None of those interviewed provided any credible leads.

On March 25, 1968, a fourth female body was discovered just a few blocks from where Joan Schell was found.

The body was that of a 16-year-old high school drop out, Maralynn Shelton, who was last seen the day before, hitchhiking in Ann Arbor. Now her nude, dead body was lying at a construction site.

Maralynn's death was much more violent than the others. The welts across her body indicated she had been brutally whipped with a leather belt, a large buckle making deep impressions on her torso and her head had also been savagely beaten. The killer or killers stuffed a piece of cloth down her throat, then posed her lying in a spread eagle position and cruelly shoved a tree branch into her vagina.

Maralynn only had one earring on, the other was missing; perhaps the killer had taken it as a souvenir, or possibly it had fallen out in his car and might later become evidence used to convict the murderer.

In a matter of a year and half, four women had been viciously murdered around the Ypsilanti and Ann Arbor area. The University of Michigan and Eastern Michigan University were advising young women to take precautions to protect themselves. Signs around campus and in town, radio and television announcements warned women not to walk alone, not to hitchhike and not to talk to or accept rides from strangers.

Several parents, out of concern for the safety of their daughters, forced them to withdraw from the universities, while many other coeds voluntarily took the semester off and went home.

The fear extended to other colleges and universities around Michigan. A killer or killers were in the state viciously murdering and mutilating young women. The schools increased their campus security and issued warnings for students to only walk in groups and not to accept rides from anyone.

The fifth victim to be found was Dawn Basom. Dawn had left a house near the Eastern Michigan campus and not been seen until the next day when her body was discovered along a country road. The body was just off the roadway, as if the killer didn't want to hide her; possibly he wanted her to be found. Her body was found with her bra and white blouse shoved up around her neck.

Dawn had been strangled with an electrical cord, a piece torn from her blouse had been stuffed in her mouth and her breasts and buttocks had been slashed viciously with a knife.

Dawn was only a 13-year-old eighth-grade student.

It was obvious to the investigators that she, as the other women, had been killed elsewhere and re-positioned along the roadside. A search of an abandoned farmhouse found Dawn's sweater, pieces ripped from her blouse, an electrical cord and a puddle of fresh blood.

Days later a subsequent search of the building revealed another piece of material torn from Dawn's blouse and one gold earring. The earring matched the earring that Maralynn Shelton had been wearing.

The police were adamant that those two items were not in the farmhouse the first time they had searched it. The killer or killers must have revisited the house and planted the items, toying with and taunting the investigators.

On June 8, 1969, three young boys discovered the body of victim number six at the edge of a farm field.

She was Alice Kalom, a graduate student enrolled at the University of Michigan's fine art's program. The 23-year-old had been seen spending time and dancing with a young man with long hair at a local club. The next day her bloody corpse was found.

She, as all the other fatalities, had been viciously slaughtered. The murderer had shot her in the head and in a rage the killer had slashed her throat.

Many in the communities of Ypsilanti and Ann Arbor thought the authorities were mishandling the crimes and that interdepartmental rivalries and squabbling were hampering the investigation. Six women had been brutally murdered in two years and the police had not arrested anyone. Women continued to die.

Some individuals, fed up with the authorities, sought donations to hire Peter Hurkos, the self proclaimed psychic who made a living entertaining audiences with his abilities.

Hurkos had made headlines when he was called in to help solve the Boston Strangler killing. The citizenry of Ann Arbor and Ypsilanti thought possibly the psychic could help solve the string of murders in their cities.

About this same time, the multiple criminal investigation units; Michigan State Police, Washtenaw County Sheriff's Department, Ypsilanti Police, Ann Arbor Police, and campus police from both universities working the crimes, united to form a single unit with the sole purpose to capture the person or persons responsible for savagely murdering the six young women.

The taskforce provided Hurkos only with information that had already been made public and was assigned three officers to escort him to the sites where the bodies had been found.

The information Peter Hurkos gave to the taskforce was said to provide some insight into the profile of the killer but other information was of no help.

The psychic announced several times that he was close and that the identification of the killer would soon be made. He did predict that the killer was a homosexual with a genius IQ. Hurkos also told police that the killer was a member of a blood cult, a salesman during the day and a student in the evening, and he liked to hang around at garbage dumps.

Hurkos described the killer as a 25-26 year old man with blond hair, about five feet seven inches tall and weighing between 136 and 146 pounds. He also said the killer was in some way associated with a trailer.

A few days later the psychic changed the description to a six-foot man with dark brown hair.

One of the only predictions the psychic Peter Hurkos made that did become a reality; he predicted the killer would soon strike again.

Just days later on July 26, 1969, the nude body of eighteen year-old Karen Sue Beineman, a freshman attending summer classes at Eastern Michigan University, was found.

The Grand Rapids native had been brutally beaten. As she lay dying, or just after her death, secretion evidence indicated the killer had raped her. The autopsy revealed the Karen Beineman's head had been severely beaten, a piece of cloth was shoved down her throat and her ripped panties had been cruelly jammed deep into her vagina.

When the panties were removed from the corpse, several unusual hairs were found on them. The hair samples were not from Karen nor were they pubic hair; they were of some other origin.

The investigators found that Ms. Beineman had last been seen three days earlier at a wig store. Karen had told the salesperson she had a ride home with a guy on a motorcycle she had just met. The clerk

*John Norman Collins in a photograph released by the police.*

recommended she change her mind and reminded Karen about the murders that had been wreaking havoc in the area. Karen Beineman did not heed the advice; she left the shop and drove on with the young man.

The sales person and several other witnesses cooperated with the police to develop a composite sketch of the man seen driving off with Karen Beineman. The sketch was published in area newspapers in hopes someone would recognize the drawing and come forth.

A campus police officer noticed the similarity between the sketch and a man he had seen riding around on his motorcycle the day Karen Beineman disappeared; John Norman Collins.

He obtained a photograph of Collins and took it to one of the witnesses who saw Ms. Beineman drive off on the motorcycle. The woman was 100% sure the man in the photograph was the same man she saw drive off with the girl who was found dead three days later.

The police officer, working on his own, approached Collins and questioned him about his activities on the day of Karen's disappearance.

The premature questioning provided John Norman Collins with time to dispose of any evidence he might still have in his possession. Collins' roommate later testified that after the questioning John left the apartment with a box covered with a blanket. Before he left, one of the roommates saw a pair of jeans, a purse and a woman's shoe in the box.

Several witnesses placed John Collins near the wig shop where Karen Beineman was last seen. The wig shop owner identified Collins as the man driving the motorcycle Karen got on, and other young women identified Collins as the man who attempted to pick them up on the same day.

John Collins had been helping out his uncle, Michigan State Police Corporal David Leik. While Corporal Leik, his wife and three sons were on vacation, John was asked to keep an eye on the house.

Upon their return, they noticed some unusual paint marks on their concrete basement floor. They were sure the paint had not been there before they went on vacation. They also found a can of paint, a box of

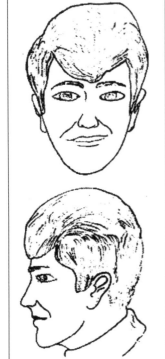

**A SEARCH IS ON** in the Ann Arbor-Ypsilanti area of Michigan for a man who resembles these drawings, made by an Ypsilanti detective from descriptions by two persons who saw murdered Karen Sue Beineman riding on the back of his motorcycle. Seven mystery slayings of girls in the area in two years preceded hers.

laundry detergent and a bottle of ammonia missing.

The missing items and paint on the floor perplexed the couple but it wasn't until they learned that their nephew was the prime suspect in the murder of six women that they suspected their house might somehow be involved in the deaths.

Mr. Leik, a Michigan State Police Trooper, wondered if something suspicious might be under the paint. He scraped away some of the paint and found a brown stain that resembled dried blood. He called the crime lab to test the stain.

The stains on the Leik basement floor turned out to be varnish. David had forgotten he had spilled varnish on the floor several years earlier. Yet, why had someone painted over stains that looked like dried blood?

The crime lab found tiny specks that looked to be dried blood and hair clippings on the floor in the basement. Mr. Leik didn't know anything about the specks but explained that his wife cuts their son's hair in the basement and it was probably from them. Samples of the hair and suspicious specks were taken.

Tests proved that the hair found on floor in the Leik basement matched the hair found on Karen Beineman's panties. The specks were tested and found to be human blood. It was the same blood type as the victim. Incriminating evidence was accumulating. The police arrested John Norman Collins for the murder of Karen Beineman.

The first attorney to represent Collins suggested that John plead guilty due to diminished capacity. Collins' mother would not agree with the recommendation and fired the lawyer.

# LAWRENCE DAILY JOURNAL-WORLD

VOL. 111, NO. 183 ★ LAWRENCE, KANSAS, FRIDAY EVENING, AUGUST 1, 1969 10 CENTS SIXTEEN PAGES

## Ypsilanti Man Arrested for Coed Slayings

The Collins trial began on June 30, 1970, with a new defense team.

The prosecution presented evidence they believed proved without a shadow of doubt that John Norman Collins had killed Karen Sue Beineman. They called the wig shop owner who testified that she saw Ms. Beineman drive away from her shop with Collins. Collins' roommate told the court about the box of women's clothing Collins had disposed of. The roommate also said that Collins asked him to provide a false alibi for the time period that Karen Beineman was killed.

Members of the crime lab testified about finding blood and hair samples in the Leik family basement. Scientists provided expert testimony that the hair found in the Leik basement was an exact match to the hair samples discovered on Ms. Beineman's panties.

The defense, in cross examination, refuted the prosecution's claims and presented expert witnesses that supported their position that John Collins could not be connected to the death of the young woman.

# The News-Palladium

Michigan's Biggest Buy . . . For Reader And For Advertiser

FINAL EDITION BENTON HARBOR, MICH. SATURDAY, AUGUST 2, 1969 20 PAGES 10c

## COLLINS: HE DOESN'T FIT 'IMAGE'

**Known As Scholar, Athlete**

'Loved Cycles Even Better Than Girls'

**Murder Suspect Arraigned**

Seek Links With Other Coed Slayings

**While Police Check Link to 6 Other Murders...**

# 'Guy Girl Could Trust'
# Held in Slaying of Coed

During the course of the trial, fifty-seven witnesses were called. In the end, the jury of six women and six men deliberated for three days and returned a verdict.

On August 19, 1970, John Norman Collins was found guilty of murdering Karen Sue Beineman.

Since Michigan law does not have a provision for a death penalty, Collins was sentenced to a minimum of 26 years before he could be considered for parole.

Collins was incarcerated at the Southern Michigan prison in Jackson, Michigan, then transferred to the Northern Michigan maximum-security prison in Marquette.

John Norman Collins continued to proclaim his innocence and was never arrested for the murders of the other five young women killed in the Ypsilanti and Ann Arbor area, or the death of a girl Collins is suspected of killing while visiting California. Yet after he was arrested, the similar deaths of young women in Michigan stopped.

The Weather
Showers tonight; warm Thursday
136th Year, No. 231

# THE ANN ARBOR NEWS

Ann Arbor, Michigan, Wednesday, August 19, 1970 ★ ★ ★ 40 Pages Plus 8, 16 Page Tabloids And 3 Page Section Supplement 10 Cents

# COLLINS FOUND GUILTY
## *Life Sentence Is Mandatory*

A Grim Collins Leaves County Building

# The Sick Mind Of Jeffery Dahmer

Wisconsin's Ed Gein will always be remembered as one of America's most bizarre murderers, but while Gein languished in the Mendota Mental Health Institute, another of America's most notorious serial killers was just getting his criminal career started.

Jeffery Dahmer was born in Milwaukee, Wisconsin, on May 21, 1960, and grew up in Iowa while his father worked on his Ph.D. at Iowa State University. In 1966 the Dahmer family moved to Akron, Ohio, where Mr. Dahmer took a job as a research chemist.

Jeffery had a normal happy childhood according to his father. But when he was six, Jeff experienced the traumatic life changing events of moving to a new city and school and the birth of his brother David. It was about this time that his father said Jeffery seemed to change. He became reclusive, preferring to stay in his room and watch TV than to socialize with his peers. He did not seem to seek out friendships but then they didn't seek his friendship either.

During his trial it came out that as a teenager Jeff had a fascination with death. He enjoyed picking up dead animals he found along the side of the road. Jeff admitted he enjoyed skinning the flesh from the animals and arranging the animal corpse in ritualistic poses. This was the beginning of Jeffery Dahmer's preoccupation with the dead, a preoccupation that would completely consume him as an adult.

Jeff graduated from high school as an average student and shortly afterward his parents, Joyce and Lionel, divorced. While Jeff was not very close to his parents, it was a period of intense emotional stress. He

didn't handle change well and the divorce was unsettling. It posed too many unanswered questions; whom would he live with? Who would care for his younger brother, 12-year-old David?

These life-changing events were traumatic to be sure but they cannot be blamed for what Jeffery Dahmer later did.

It was in June of 1978 when an eighteen-year-old Jeffery picked up a hitchhiker, Steve Hicks. While driving, the two talked and hit it off and Jeff invited him back to his parent's house for a beer. They drank beer and later engaged in homosexual sex acts.

This was Jeff's first actual sexual experience with another male. He admitted to thinking about it since he was about 14 years old but never acted on his desires.

The evening Jeff spent with the hitchhiker was an awakening for Jeff, a dream come true. But for Jeff, the dream became a nightmare when Steve Hicks wanted to leave.

Dahmer tried to reason with him, tried to convince him to stay, but Steve wanted to leave.

The thought of his new friend, his sex partner, his dream come true leaving was too much for the 18-year-old Jeffery Dahmer to bear. In a fit of rage, Jeffery picked up a steel barbell and struck Steve in the head killing him almost instantly.

Jeff was thrilled with the events of the evening; picking up a strange man, having sex with him, and then the biggest thrill... killing him. But

*An early mug shot of Jeffery Dahmer from the Milwaukee Police Department.*

when he returned to reality, he realized he had to dispose of the body. He couldn't just leave a corpse of a dead man in his parent's basement. He had to get rid of the body of a fully-grown man without his father or new stepmother finding out.

Slowly and methodically, Jeff used a knife to hack Steve's body into smaller pieces. He packed them in garbage bags and twist tied them closed. Jeff carried the bags out one or two at a time during the night and buried them in the woods behind the house.

Afterward, Jeffery's mind was a mass of confused feelings. He enjoyed the homosexual sex and reveled in reminiscing about it and fantasizing about future encounters, but he wondered why he didn't harbor guilty feelings for killing the hitchhiker. Instead it brought about intense sexual excitement.

Jeff spent the rest of the summer in an alcohol-induced daze. He didn't have a job, he just sat around the house watching TV and drinking. Perhaps he was trying to dull the evil thoughts that filled his very existence.

His parents, tired of his constant drinking and laziness, made him enroll in college. They thought possibly the world of academia would agree with Jeff and turn his life around.

In the fall of 1978, Jeffery enrolled as a freshman at Ohio State University. He drank almost constantly, attended classes irregularly and flunked out after one semester.

Jeffery's next step in life was yet another failure. After flunking out of college, his father and stepmother would not tolerate him sitting around drinking all of the time. So late in 1978 he joined the United States Army.

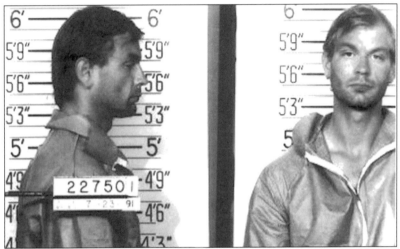

*A mug shot of Jeffery Dahmer after his arrest for the murders of 17 Milwaukee men.*

According to police investigators who met with Jeffery at a later point of his life, Jeffery held his strange and twisted desires in check while he was in the Army stationed in Germany. A thorough investigation by German authorities did not find any link between Dahmer and murders that occurred while he was stationed there.

As with the rest of his life, Jeff's military career was less than illustrious. After two years, Dahmer was discharged from the Army for his excessive use of alcohol. Jeffery's alcoholism forced major changes in his life; he flunked out of college and he was kicked out of the Army.

After being discharged from the Army, Jeff went to Florida for a bit but ended up back in Ohio living with his parents, which was also the scene of his first murder.

Jeffery could not get the thought of killing Steve Hicks out of his demented mind. He dwelled on the thought of the dismembered corpse of the hitchhiker buried in his parent's backyard. Once home, he made a midnight trip out to the yard and dug up the plastic bags. He opened the bags with macabre interest; he had been dreaming about the decomposing body.

After viewing the hitchhikers remains, Jeff was fascinated with the extent of the rotting and putrefied body parts. Dahmer used a sledgehammer to smash the remains into small parts, pulverizing the bones. He then scattered the small parts of Steven Hicks throughout the woods to be consumed and carried away by small animals.

Fed up with his son, Lionel Dahmer made arrangements for Jeff to live with his grandmother in West Allis, Wisconsin, a suburb of Milwaukee. Jeffery found a job working in a chocolate factory and he seemed to be keeping his demons at bay.

That was until he was arrested for two sexually explicit crimes. He was caught dropping his pants in front of a group of strangers. Then he was arrested again in 1986 for masturbating in front of two young boys.

This behavior should have been a signal for mental health officials that they were dealing with a man with severe emotional problems but the judge hearing the case only gave Jeff one year probation for his lewd act in front of the two boys.

One year after being sentenced to probation, Jeffery Dahmer's life spun out of control. In September of 1987, Jeff met Steve Toumi in a Milwaukee gay bar. The two men left the bar together and went to a local motel. They drank, had sex and fell asleep.

In the morning, still in an alcohol induced fog, Dahmer awoke to find Toumi laying next to him. Steve Toumi was dead. Dahmer later told detectives that he didn't know how Toumi had died but he knew he had to dispose of the body. Calmly, Jeff went to a store and purchased the largest suitcase he could find. Back at the motel he folded and stuffed Steve Toumi's body into the suitcase.

Jeffery could have thrown the suitcase into a dumpster or sunk it in Lake Michigan, but he took the body back to his grandmother's house to satisfy his perverse fascination with death and dead bodies. Jeffery Dahmer wasn't yet done with the corpse of Steve Toumi.

Once back at his grandmother's basement, Dahmer would realize some of his deep dark desires. He posed the body, fondled it, and had sex with the dead man's corpse.

Jeff didn't want to get rid of the body, he kept it for awhile to fulfill his depraved sexual needs with a slowly decomposing corpse.

After sedating his strange sexual desires, he dismembered Steve Toumi's body, placed the pieces in garbage bags and distributed them into garbage containers around the city.

Just over a month later Dahmer struck again. He met a fourteen-year-old Native American boy, Jamie Doxtator, outside a Milwaukee gay bar. Jeffery lured the boy to his grandmother's basement where the boy was drugged. As the boy lay on the couch, Jeffery slowly wrapped his fingers around the boy's throat and began to squeeze until Jamie had taken his last breath. As Dahmer had done with his last victim, Jeff had sex with the dead corpse of the young boy, cut the boy into manageable sized pieces and disposed of the body parts.

Jeff sought out other victims by cruising gay bars and bathhouses of Milwaukee where he found his next prey, Richard Guerrero. Richard met with the same fate as the other victims, drugged, killed, raped, dismembered, and disposed.

Jeffery Dahmer had killed four people, but he had no remorse, no guilt, rather his own sexual need dominated his life. After fulfilling his desires, the only thing important to Dahmer was not being caught.

Dahmer was killing and dismembering men in his grandmother's basement! It was time for him to get an apartment of his own where he could carry on with his demented and depraved life. His grandmother was ready for Jeff to leave anyway, not because she knew what was happening in her basement, but she was tired of Jeff bringing home his friends, the drinking and all of the noise coming from the basement.

He found an apartment he could afford in the crime-ridden section of Milwaukee near Marquette University. He moved to 924 North 25th Street, apartment 213 in the Oxford Apartments. In his second floor apartment he could carry on his ghoulish ways with less chance of being detected.

For the next two and half years Jeffery Dahmer worked at the chocolate factory by day and by night visited bathhouses and bars. During the time he lived at the Oxford Apartments, Dahmer followed his proven method of seducing men or boys by offering them drinks, money for posing for photographs, or inviting them to watch sexually explicit videos.

In May of 1991 Dahmer was careless and was almost caught by the Milwaukee Police. Two eighteen-year-old women called 911 at 2:00 am to report a drunk boy wandering around completely nude. They also reported that a blonde white man was trying to get the boy to go to his apartment.

Police and paramedics arrived and checked the boy over, while Jeff Dahmer calmly explained to the police that the boy was actually his 19-year-old lover who had too much to drink. Jeff told the officers that he would take him home and let him sleep it off.

The two girls had seen the look of fear on the boy's face when Jeff was trying to get him back to his apartment. They tried to tell the police that the boy didn't want to go with the blonde man. They pleaded with the police not to allow the blonde man to take the boy.

The police decided to escort the two men back to the apartment to see if there was a relationship between the two as Dahmer had said.

In the police report it was stated that the second floor apartment was neat and clean but had a rancid odor as if garbage was rotting in it. Dahmer produced photographs of the boy Jeff claimed was 19-years-old. The photographs showed the boy smiling and posing in a black bikini.

Jeff apologized for the trouble his lover had caused and promised that it wouldn't happen again. The police were reluctant to become involved with the homosexual lovers since there didn't seem to be anything more to the story other than what Dahmer had explained.

After the police left, Jeffery was furious with how close his young lover had come to getting him caught. He walked up to the dazed boy sitting on the couch, placed his hands around the boy's throat and slowly tightened his grip until there was no movement, no sign of life coming from the 14-year-old boy.

Jeffery Dahmer continued his murderous ways, killing another 12 men and boys while he lived at the Oxford Apartment.

On a hot July 22, 1991 evening, two Milwaukee police officers were patrolling the area near Marquette University when they observed a black man stumbling down the street with a set of handcuffs dangling from one wrist. Suspecting the man might have escaped from another police officer, they pulled up to the man and ordered him to stop. The man readily complied; he was not running from the police, rather he was looking for them.

The man began rambling on about a blonde guy who had handcuffed him and threatened him with a knife. The police followed the man to apartment 213 at the Oxford Apartments to check out his story.

A clean cut, well-spoken, white man answered their knock and the two officers and the handcuffed man were invited in. Officer Rolf Mueller noticed the apartment was neat and clean but it stunk of rotting garbage. The putrid smell was almost un-bearable, but an apartment smelling of garbage was not unusual in this neighborhood.

Thirty-one-year-old Jeffery Dahmer explained that there was nothing sinister going on; it was just a sex game that he and the man enjoyed playing. Jeff offered to get the key to the set of handcuffs from his bedroom.

The black man protested that the knife he was threatened with was in the bedroom so the officer told Jeff to stay where he was and he would go into the bedroom to retrieve the key. It was a decision that would send shockwaves across the country and around the world.

In the bedroom the officer noticed a large quantity of photographs lying around the room. He picked up several and was amazed at what he saw: a dead dismembered body, skulls, and photographs of human heads in a refrigerator.

"Cuff him!" the police officer yelled to his partner standing with Jeff Dahmer.

Dahmer's calm and cooperative demeanor immediately changed. He began to struggle with the police; it took both officers to subdue Dahmer.

Once Dahmer was cuffed Officer Mueller went to the kitchen, the refrigerator looked similar to the one he saw in the photograph. He opened he door. Even though he suspected what he might find, he was still not prepared for it. He looked in and a severed man's head stared back at him.

Jeffery Dahmer was taken to the police station and investigators swarmed apartment 213. What they were about to discover would be recorded as one of the most horrific crimes ever to occur in the United States.

The forensic investigators discovered, in addition to the head in the refrigerator, three more human heads wrapped in plastic bags in the freezer compartment. On a closet shelf in Dahmer's bedroom were two human skulls, painted gray. Other of Dahmer's macabre collection included formaldehyde-filled jars preserving several male penises.

# The Sick Mind Of Jeffery Dahmer

To remember and relive his grizzly murders, Dahmer took hundreds of photographs of his victims. The photographs illustrated male bodies in various stages of dismemberment.

In his own warped way, Dahmer performed medical experiments on some of his victims. He drilled holes in the heads of drugged men and boys then poured muratic acid into their brains. Dahmer said he was trying to create a zombie that would be his slave forever. The victims of course died.

In an act of ultimate control over his prey, Dahmer engaged in acts of cannibalism. Found in the freezer along with the heads were several freezer bags of human flesh.

Dahmer confessed that he would skin the men as a hunter would skin a deer. The biceps and other muscles would be wrapped and frozen so Dahmer could eat them later. Dahmer admitted he experimented with various spices and meat tenderizers in an effort to make the meat more palpable.

As crime investigators, dressed in yellow biohazard suits, removed bags of decaying body parts from the apartment, neighbors in the building talked to reporters.

One neighbor told the Associated Press, "We've been smelling odors for weeks, but we thought it was a dead animal or something like that. We had no idea it was humans."

Another neighbor who lived below Dahmer in the Oxford Apartments related, "We heard sawing coming from the apartment upstairs at all hours of the day and night." They wondered what the guy upstairs was building.

While the ghastly contents of Dahmer's apartment were being uncovered and cataloged by the forensic scientists, Jeffery Dahmer was openly talking to Detective Patrick Kennedy of the Milwaukee Police Department.

Dahmer related how he would meet the men and boys at locations frequented by Milwaukee's gay population. He talked about inviting the men back to his apartment for drinks or offered them money to pose for photographs and sometimes the men accompanied Dahmer at an invitation to watch homosexual videos.

Dahmer then described to Detective Kennedy in detail how he drugged the men with prescription medications prescribed to Dahmer. He ground the pills up and put it in their drinks. He next told the

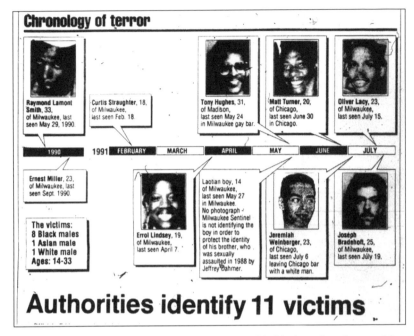

## Chronology of terror

**Raymond Lamont Smith, 33,** of Milwaukee, last seen May 29, 1990.

**Curtis Straughter, 18,** of Milwaukee, last seen Feb. 18.

**Tony Hughes, 31,** of Madison, last seen May 24 in Milwaukee gay bar.

**Matt Turner, 20,** of Chicago, last seen June 30 in Chicago.

**Oliver Lacy, 23,** of Milwaukee, last seen July 15.

1990    1991   FEBRUARY   MARCH   APRIL   MAY   JUNE   JULY

**Ernest Miller, 23,** of Milwaukee, last seen Sept. 1990.

**The victims:**
8 Black males
1 Asian male
1 White male
Ages: 14-33

**Errol Lindsey, 19,** of Milwaukee, last seen April 7.

Laotian boy, 14 of Milwaukee, last seen May 27 in Milwaukee. No photograph - Milwaukee Sentinel is not identifying the boy in order to protect the identity of his brother, who was sexually assaulted in 1988 by Jeffrey Dahmer.

**Jeremiah Weinberger, 23,** of Chicago, last seen July 6 leaving Chicago bar with a white man.

**Joseph Bradehoft, 25,** of Milwaukee, last seen July 19.

## Authorities identify 11 victims

detective how he would strangle the men with his bare hands or with a leather belt.

Under Detective Kennedy's gentle probing, Dahmer calmly admitted to having sex with the bodies; sometimes he would have anal sex with the corpse of the dead men and boys or other times he enjoyed masturbating on their bodies.

Dahmer volunteered to the detective how he would cut open the bodies, sometimes skin them or other times he would dismember the bodies and melt the flesh off the bones with caustic chemicals then flush the sludge down the drain.

A large pot was found in Jeffery Dahmer's closet filled with his flesh eating concoction. Soaking in the pot were several of his victim's hands and another of Jeffery's souvenirs… a penis.

Dahmer described in detail how he soaked two skulls in the vat of acid to remove the flesh from the bone. He cleaned the skull, dried it and painted them gray. He envisioned using the skulls in a shrine; a shrine where only he would worship the evil thoughts that abounded in his head.

He was reluctant to talk about eating the flesh of his victims but once he admitted it, he started talking. He told Detective Kennedy how he would cut the muscle and other fleshy parts from the men he killed. Then slice it into thin portions. Jeffery told how he enjoyed the texture of the fresh meat in his hands and how he would fry some of it. Some of the "meat" he froze for later consumption. He also confessed to drinking the blood of some of the men he murdered but said it was just not something he enjoyed.

Jeffery Dahmer was arraigned in Milwaukee District Court on charges of murder. Because his crimes were so heinous and he was so hated, a bullet resistant shield was constructed between Dahmer and the gallery, one to keep the murderer away from the gallery and two to keep the people in the gallery away from the murderer.

The defense team representing Jeffery Dahmer entered an innocent plea. They claimed that despite his confession he was not guilty of the murders that occurred in his apartment. But, on July 13, 1992, Dahmer changed his plea, against the wishes of his legal team, to guilty but insane.

The nature of the trial changed for both the defense and the prosecution. Now the defense would have to bring out all of the grotesque details of what Dahmer had done to prove he must be insane, and the prosecution team had to change their tack from proving that Dahmer had killed the men to proving that he was sane when he killed them.

Two Milwaukee Police Detectives took the stand taking turns reading Dahmer's 160-page confession. Both sides produced psychologists to support their case. Forensic scientists were called to testify about the macabre scene they found at apartment 213 of the Oxford Apartments.

They told of the human "meat" found in the freezer, the skulls in the closet, the hands and penises soaking in a vat of acid. The forensic scientists told the court of all of the depravity they had discovered in the world of Jeffery Dahmer.

The jury sat through the grotesque testimony and received instructions from the judge to return with a verdict; was Jeffery Dahmer guilty of 15 counts of murder and various other charges relating to mutilation of a corpse, and other such charges and be sentenced to life imprisonment.

# How many bodies? Who?
Behind the stench was a gruesome collection

Pharos-Tribune, Logansport, Indiana, Friday, December 16, 1994

# Suspect Says God Ordered Dahmer's Death

Or was Jeffery Dahmer insane during his 13-year murder spree and should he be sent to a hospital for the criminally insane for the remainder of his life.

The jury only took five hours to return a verdict of guilty and sane. Jeffery Dahmer received a sentence of 15 life terms for fifteen of the men he killed.

For his thirteen year rein of evilness, Dahmer was sent to the Columbia Correctional Institute in Portage, Wisconsin, for the next 957 years or the duration of his life, which ever came first.

Jeffery Dahmer, the worst serial killer in Wisconsin's history and one of the worst in the nation, did not serve 957 years for on November 28, 1994, prisoner Christopher Scarver beat Jeffery Dahmer to death with a broom handle, thus ending the horrific existence of Jeffery Dahmer.

## Victims of Jeffery Dahmer

| Name | Year of Death |
| --- | --- |
| Steven Hicks | 1978 |
| Steven Tourmi | 1987 |
| Jamie Doxtator | 1988 |
| Richard Guerrero | 1988 |
| Anthony Sears | 1989 |
| Edward Smith | 1990 |
| Ricky Lee Beeks | 1990 |
| Ernest Miller | 1990 |
| David Thomas | 1990 |
| Curtis Straughter | 1991 |
| Errol Lindsey | 1991 |
| Anthony Hughes | 1991 |
| Konerak Sinthasomphone | 1991 |
| Matt Turner | 1991 |
| Jeremiah Weinberger | 1991 |
| Oliver Lacey | 1991 |
| Joe Bradehoft | 1991 |

# The Interstate Murderers - Coleman And Brown

Alton Coleman was a man who was driven by his emotions and sexual appetite. He was a true sociopath, for he had no remorse, no feeling for the people he used for his own gratification.

His parents left him to live with his grandmother, and growing up he suffered horribly embarrassing nicknames because he had a weak bladder and often urinated in his pants. Alton acted out in school and on the streets. By the time he dropped out of middle school, he had a long relationship with the Waukegan, Illinois police.

Neighbors remember Alton as a troubled little boy. Classmates and friends remember Alton was obsessed with sex.

In 1983, Alton met a young woman, Debra Brown. Brown was described as mentally challenged but she had never been in trouble with the police. Alton and Debra were instantly attracted to one another and Debra fell so deeply in love with Coleman that she left her fiance and moved in with Alton.

They were not good for each other. Debra worshiped Alton. She would do anything he wanted. Pleasing Alton was the most important thing to her. She went along with anything he said and did. With Alton's powerful sexual drive, he demanded more and different sexual experiences and she eagerly complied. She wanted to make Alton happy, no matter what it took.

Debra and Alton fed off each other's weaknesses, her desire to please her man and his overpowering sexual appetite. In 1984, this led the couple to go on a summer long crime spree that would take them to six Midwest states.

Coleman met a young single mother, Juanita Wheat, who lived in Kenosha, Wisconsin. He and Debra often drove from their home in Waukegan, Illinois, to visit Juanita and her nine-year-old daughter, Vernita. Juanita considered the young couple to be friends. She didn't suspect anything and on one visit, Alton and Debra abducted Vernita, drove back to Waukegan, sexually molested the child and killed her.

Weeks later in an abandoned building in Waukegan, Illinois, the decomposing body of nine-year-old Vernita was discovered. The child had been strangled.

The Bonnie and Clyde "wannabe's" next befriended a man in Waukegan and spent the evening with him eating dinner and drinking. The young couple then stole his car. He was fortunate they only took his car and he was lucky they didn't take his life.

The murderous duo drove the Waukegan man's car to nearby Gary, Indiana, where Alton's perverse desires again drove the couple to rape and murder. In Gary, they found two young sisters: nine-year-old Annie and seven-year-old Tamika Turks.

Several days later the body of little Tamika was found. Her small body was already decomposing in the summer's heat. The little girl had been raped and strangled. Despite being subjected to the same heinous crimes, nine-year-old Annie lived through the ordeal. She told the police of the man and woman who had both performed sexual acts on her and her sister then strangled them. Annie was left for dead. This was the first indication that Debra was a willing participant in the rapes and murders.

On July 11, 1984, a dead body was found in Detroit, Michigan. Although the corpse was badly decomposed, the police were able to identify the body to be that of 25-year-old Donna Williams. Ms. Williams had been missing from her Gary, Indiana, home for almost a month. She had been molested and strangled. Alton and Debra had taken her from her home to Detroit.

The perverted murderers traveled west of Detroit to the suburb of Dearborn Heights where they randomly selected a house, the house of Mr. and Mrs. Palmer Jones. Coleman and Brown handcuffed and tied up the Jones' then brutally beat them. Brown and Coleman then stole their money and car. The Jones had met the devils from Illinois. They were severely beaten but they were alive.

The next Midwestern state Alton and Debra were to visit was Ohio. In Toledo, the two murderers befriended Virginia Temple, a single mother with five children.

Relatives of the Temple family grew concerned that they hadn't heard from the family and went to the house to check on them.

Knocks on the door went unanswered. They let themselves in and found four of the children, all under the age of 7, alone. They were dirty and hungry. The children didn't know where their mother or their older sister, nine-year-old Rachelle, were. They had not seen them for a couple of days since the "man and woman" left.

The relatives, worried for the well being of the missing woman and girl, began to search the house. They made a grizzly discovery in the crawl space below the house, the dead bodies of Virginia and her nine-year-old daughter. Brown and Coleman had raped and killed their fourth and fifth victims.

Coleman and his obedient girlfriend again randomly selected the home of Frank and Dorothy

*Alton Coleman. From the Ohio Department Of Corrections.*

Duvendack in Toledo. As they had done in Dearborn Heights, Michigan,

Brown and Coleman pulled the phone cord from the wall and electrical cords from appliances to bind their two captives. They stole money and a car but for some unknown reason the murderers did not harm them. The Duvendack's would thank the Lord that they were not added to the list of Coleman and Brown's victims.

Dayton, Ohio, was the next stop for the murderers. In Dayton, Alton and Debra went to the house of Reverend Gay. The minister took in the travelers, fed them and drove them to a religious service in Cincinnati, Ohio. The couple were dropped off in downtown Cincinnati and the Reverend and his wife drove back to Dayton oblivious that they had just spent two days with two cold-blooded killers. A higher power had been watching over them.

With five people dead and several severely beaten in five different states, the Federal Bureau of Investigation, on July 12, 1984, placed Alton Coleman on their list of Ten Most Wanted as a special addition.

On the next day, the killers went to Norwood, Ohio. They saw a camper for sale at the home of Harry and Marlene Walters. Alton knocked at the door to inquire about the camper. Harry Walters invited them into his house to discuss the merits of the camper.

Coleman picked up a candle holder pretending to admire it, then, without provocation, slammed it down on the back of Mr. Walters head with such force it drove pieces of Harry's skull into his brain.

When Harry and Marlene's daughter came home from work she found the walls of the house splattered with blood. She searched the house and found her mother and father lying at the bottom of the basement stairs. The murderers had savagely beaten the couple and tossed them down the stairs.

Mrs. Walters laid on the cold concrete floor, a blood soaked sheet wrapped around her head and her hands and feet bound with electrical cords. The coroner estimated Marlene had been struck in the head 20 to 25 times and the back of her skull was in fragments. There were also twelve lacerations to her face, some caused by being struck with a pair of vice grip pliers. She had not survived the ordeal.

Harry, like his wife, had been beaten, tied up, strangled, and left for dead. Harry miraculously lived through the nightmare.

The murder was the most brutal thus far, but evidence of who was responsible was found. Shards of glass from a pop bottle that broke as it crushed in Marlene's skull were found to contain bloody fingerprints. The fingerprints were those of Alton Coleman.

Brown and Coleman took the Walter's car, money, clothes, shoes, watch, and jewelry.

The Walter's car was found abandoned in Kentucky where the killers kidnapped a college professor, Oline Carmichael. They forced Professor Carmichael into the trunk of his car and drove back to Dayton, Ohio.

Alton and Debra abandoned the car with Carmichael locked in the trunk. He was able to alert a passerby and authorities released him from the trunk. The Dayton Police now knew that the pair of violent and vicious murderers, who were the subject of a nationwide search, were in their town.

Alton and Debra went to the familiar home of Reverend Gay. The Reverend and his wife now knew the nice strangers they had taken to a church service were the sadistic killers leaving a path of pain and death across the Midwest. They begged the killers not to hurt them. Alton told them that they weren't going to kill them, but they usually do. They beat the 79-year-old Reverend and stole his car.

On their trip back to Illinois, the murderous couple realized that the police would be looking for the Reverend's car. In route, they overpowered a 77-year-old man, killed him and took his car.

Back in Waukegan, Illinois, Coleman and Brown laid low. They knew local, state and federal authorities were hunting them. They were trying not to attract attention to themselves.

On July 20, 1984, a man who knew them, saw Coleman and Brown walking across a street in Waukegan. He drove to a gas station and called the police.

The Waukegan Police swarmed to the area. They observed a man and woman sitting on a set of bleachers at a city park. As two officers approached, Debra Brown got up and began calmly walking away into the park.

The police stopped Alton and began to question him. He did not have any identification and denied being Alton Coleman. Other officers stopped Brown. When searched, they found a gun in Brown's purse. Both Alton and Brown, two vicious and violent killers, were taken into custody without any resistance.

The young couple from Waukegan could not control their perverse urges. For selfish thrills, they raped and killed seven men, women and

children and kidnapped and/or beat seven more. The victims of the murderous couple included; nine-year-old Vernita Wheat, seven-year-old Tamika Turks, Debra Williams, Virginia Temple, nine-year-old Rachelle Temple, Marlene Walters, and a 77-year-old man.

After the arrest, authorities from Michigan, Wisconsin, Illinois, Ohio, Indiana and Kentucky met to determine how they would proceed with prosecuting Brown and Coleman. Each state had enough evidence to take the killing couple to trial. Michigan was ruled out as the primary trial since the state does not have a death penalty for murder. The prosecutors wanted the most severe penalty possible for Alton Coleman and Debra Brown. It was decided that the first trial would be held in Ohio for the savage beating death of Marlene Walters. Alton Coleman was found guilty and sentenced to death.

Alton Coleman was also found guilty and sentenced to death in Illinois and Indiana for murders committed in those states.

Debra Brown was found guilty of the murders and received a similar sentence.

In 1991, the governor of Ohio commuted Debra Brown's death penalty to life in prison and she is still incarcerated without the possibility of parole in the Ohio Reformatory for Women.

Alton Coleman sent a deluge of appeals to the Ohio judicial system in an effort to delay his execution. But in April of 2001, the murdering, sexually obsessed Alton Coleman was put to death by lethal injection.

# All My Best, Belle - Belle Gunness

Less than 60 miles separates Chicago and La Porte, Indiana, but in the late 1800s, the two cities were a world apart. Chicago was a bustling city on the verge of worldwide prominence and La Porte was a quiet farming community. Crime was rampant in Chicago but in La Porte what crime there was, would be considered insignificant in Chicago. That was until America's most prolific female serial killer was discovered living on a farm outside La Porte, Indiana.

On November 22, 1859, a baby girl, Brynhild Paulsdatter Storset, was born in the small Norwegian village of Selbu. Her parents were poor laborers and at an early age the young girl had to take jobs working on farms as a milkmaid to help support the family.

Brynhild's sister, Nellie Larson, had immigrated with her husband to the United States and Brynhild was determined to move there as well. She saved her money and at 22 years old was able to join her sister in the "land of opportunity," Chicago, Illinois.

Brynhild found that life in the United States was not as easy as she had heard. She "Americanized" her name to Belle but the only employment she could find was work as a servant to the wealthy. She worked long hours, the rich people very demanding, and the pay was minimal.

Belle found employment as a servant but wanted more out of life. She was not content waiting on the rich; she wanted to be rich and have others wait on her.

In 1884, Belle married a young department store detective, Max Sorenson. He was a hard worker and shortly after their marriage was

hired by the Chicago & Northwestern Railroad. It was a promotion for Max, but his earnings were still not enough to keep Belle in a manner in which she desired.

To help with household expenses, Belle opened a small candy store. But the store was a minimally successful venture. Unfortunately, Belle said a kerosene lamp exploded and the building caught fire and was destroyed. The insurance company investigated and thought the fire might be suspicious but paid off the claim to Belle and Max Sorenson.

The Sorensons moved out of the city and purchased a home. In a little more than a year the home was destroyed by fire. Again a claim was made on the insurance company and Max and Belle received a cash payment.

Belle gave birth to four children, Caroline, Axel, Myrtle and Lucy while she was married to Max. Unfortunately Caroline and Axel died in infancy. The cause of death was acute colitis, a disease that has symptoms very similar to the symptoms of being poisoned. The children were insured.

In July of 1900, Max died. The first doctor who treated Max suspected that he might have died of strychnine poisoning, but Max and Belle's family doctor said he had been treating Max for an enlarged heart and that he must have died from a cardiac episode. Earlier Belle had decided to cancel a life insurance policy on Max and purchase another. The two policies overlapped for one day. Oddly, Max died on the only date that both life insurance policies were in effect. Belle was paid by both policies.

At that time Belle opted to take her two young daughters and an orphan girl she had taken in, Jennie Olson, and move away from Chicago. Belle purchased a farm with a large house on the outskirts of La Porte, Indiana.

The house was originally built by a founder of the city and over the years had been purchased by several other owners. It was even once used as a brothel. During that period a carriage house and boat house were built for the relaxation of the male customers who traveled from Chicago to enjoy the country life.

Shortly after Belle purchased the property, both the boathouse and carriage house were devastated by fire. Luckily for Belle she had insurance on the buildings.

Belle was lonely after the premature death of her husband Max. She met a widower from La Porte, Peter Gunness, and they were soon married. Belle readily accepted Peter's infant daughter into her family, although the infant must have been sickly for records show that the child died just after the couple was married.

After less than a year of marriage, Belle was once again a grieving widow. An auger from a sausage grinder fell from a shelf. Unfortunately for Peter, he was standing under it and it struck him on the head. His skull was split open. Peter's death was found to be accidental and Belle received a settlement from the life insurance company that held the policy on Peter. Belle was named as the sole beneficiary.

Before his death Peter left Belle with child. Phillip was born after his father's death.

The widow was apparently lonely and placed advertisements in Norwegian newspapers published in America. Her advertisements described her as the owner of a beautiful farm in a good community who was looking for a man to partner with her. The lonely Indiana widow told the men they would need to provide some financial assistance to become a partner in the farm. There was apparently no shortage of men willing to communicate with the widow and visit the farm with cash in hand. Neighbors reported seeing many men in their middle years, arrive at the farm but they did not remember seeing the men leave. When Belle was questioned about the men she would say the men were called away and left during the night.

Similarly the teenaged orphan who was a ward under Belle's care one day was no longer at the farm. Belle explained that Jennie Olsen had been sent to California where she was attending a Lutheran college.

*Belle Gunness. Author's Collection.*

One man, Andrew Helgelein, exchanged several letters with the Indiana widow. She convinced him to sell his belongings and travel to La Porte. He told his brother, Asle, about the correspondence and possible romance and that he was moving to Indiana to become a partner with Belle Gunness on her farm.

Several months went by without Asle hearing from his brother. Worried that possibly Andrew had met with foul play while in route and carrying $3,000.00, Asle wrote to Belle inquiring of his brother.

A reply from Belle informed Asle that Andrew had been there but he had left La Porte and moved back to Norway. Asle did not believe what the woman had written. He knew his brother, and Andrew would not leave the country without telling him. Asle, suspicious of Belle, decided to go to La Porte to confront the woman and find his brother.

Four days before Asle arrived in La Porte there was a terrible fire at the farm owned by Belle Gunness. On April 28, 1908, the house burned to the ground. While workmen sifted through the ashes, a grizzly discovery was made. Four bodies, three children and one adult female had perished in the configuration.

The bodies were all burned beyond recognition, but it had to be the bodies of Belle and her three children, eleven-year-old Myrtle, nine-year-old Lucy and son, Peter, age five.

After investigating the fire, Sheriff Albert Smutzer found the fire and deaths of the family suspicious. He determined the fire began at 4:00 am when everyone in the house should have been sleeping. Another thing that disturbed the sheriff was that the family's piano had fallen from the parlor on the ground floor into the basement as the first floor burned. However, the bodies were found beneath the burnt remains of the piano. At 4:00 am they should have been in their beds, not in the basement.

How could the victims be found beneath the piano unless their bodies were first placed in the basement?

More evidence was leading the sheriff to suspect that the fire was no accident. The day before the house burned, Belle had visited a lawyer to make out a will. She left all of her worldly belongings first to her children and if they did not survive her then her estate was to be given to a Chicago orphanage. Belle also told the lawyer that she was afraid of an ex-handyman, Ray Lamphere, who had worked on her farm. She told the lawyer that Ray had made threats to kill her and burn the house.

Ray Lamphere was questioned about the fire and arrested after a witness came forward claiming they had seen Lamphere leaving the burning house.

Lamphere had worked on the Gunness farm for a period and it was rumored that he and Belle had a relationship. When Belle fired him, he began to harass her. She went as far as requesting a sanity hearing for Lamphere. The hearing found him to be sane, although, just days later Lamphere was arrested for trespassing on the Gunness farm.

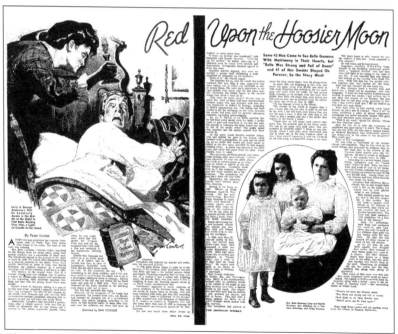

*The story of Belle Gunness was serialized in newspapers across the nation.*

While the investigation continued, Asle Helgelein showed up in town to find his brother. He talked to the sheriff and was told about the fire that destroyed the Gunness farm and killed four people. Asle asked for permission to search the farm for his missing brother.

On a hint from a farmhand that worked the Gunness farm, Asle and Sheriff Smutzer started digging. Down just four feet they found the remains of Andrew Helgelein.

More digging revealed the body of Jennie Olson, the young orphan girl left in the care of Belle Gunness. Twelve other bodies and many parts of others were discovered buried around the farm. Authorities estimate that as many as forty men were killed by Belle Gunness and disposed of on the farm.

Ray Lamphere was convicted of burning the Gunness house but not of killing the woman and three children found in the ashes. On his deathbed he confessed that he helped Belle bury the bodies of the men who visited her, but she had killed them all. He said she would poison them, hit them in the head with a meat cleaver and dismember the bodies. Lamphere would then dig the hole and place the bodies or body parts in and cover them with lye to speed the decomposition.

He also said it was not Belle's body found in the house after the fire. It was the body of a servant Belle had recently hired from Chicago. Belle had killed the woman and her three children and arranged them in the basement.

After the murders, Lamphere took Belle to a neighboring town where she boarded a train to Chicago. Then he returned to La Porte and set the house on fire.

Belle Gunness got away.

Research has shown that female serial killers poison their victims 80% of the time and in 74% of all cases the motive is money. Belle Gunness fits the profile; she poisoned her victims and was a serial killer who killed for one reason, money. She craved the finer things in life and she would do anything to get them, even kill her husbands and her own children.

# Chicago's Infamous St. Valentine's Day Massacre

One of America's most infamous criminals rose to power in Chicago, Illinois; Alphonse Gabriel Capone.

Born in 1899 in Brooklyn, New York, young Al Capone grew up in a world of crime. As a child he was involved in youth gangs and graduated to become involved with the crime families who wielded so much power there was little local police could do.

Al Capone was a tough guy. It is reputed Al had killed two gangsters, but not enough evidence was found to bring him up on charges. A bit later he severely beat a rival gang member, but before he was arrested Al was sent to Chicago and set up with a job working for "Papa" Johnny Torrio, the notorious Chicago gangster.

At that time, Johnny Torrio's South Side Italian Gang was locked in a bloody battle with the North Side Irish Gang run by Dion O'Banion for control of bootlegging and other rackets in the city. Torrio ordered the assassination of O'Banion, which set off an all out war for control of the city.

One day in November of 1924, three men walked into the flower shop owned by O'Banion. He greeted them with a smile and they greeted him with pistols. Dion O'Banion's death was just the beginning of the war between the gangs that would last for over four years and result in forty murders; forty that are known as there are probably many more that went unnoticed by the police.

Mr. Torrio was impressed with Al's intelligence, brawn and fearlessness. He promoted Al to supervise the gang's bootlegging business, a position ranking number 2 in the gang's hierarchy.

In retaliation for the murder of O'Banion, North Side gang members ambushed and nearly killed Johnny Torrio. Torrio survived the attack but decided to retire and move out of Chicago. It was Al Capone who assumed the leadership of the gang. Under his direction, the organization's saloons, speakeasies, nightclubs, bookie joints, gambling houses, prostitution houses, racetracks, breweries and distilleries thrived. But the war with the North Siders was also kept hot with several more murders by both sides.

Al Capone handled any opposition to his iron fist rule in a very definitive way. He had them killed on the street outside their home or they disappeared never to be seen again. It was said that Al Capone was responsible for ordering the deaths of dozens of men during his reign as Chicago's underworld king. However he was never convicted of any of the deaths.

Keeping the war between the two Chicago area gangs burning hot, Capone ordered the death of Earl "Hymie" Weiss who had taken control of the North Siders.

In October of 1926, Weiss and four companions were walking down the street, ironically just feet from O'Banion's flower shop when machine gun fire rang out in ambush leaving Weiss and one of his bodyguards dead and his lawyer severely wounded.

Following Weiss's death, a twenty-seven-year-old mobster named Vincent Drucci rose to power. He was unlike any of his predecessors;

# Chicago's Infamous St. Valentine's Day Massacre

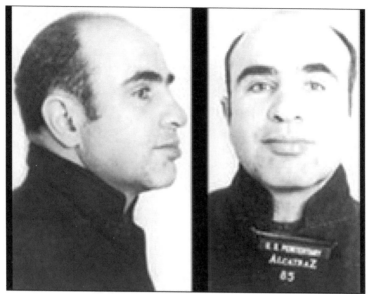

*A mug shot of a young Alphonse Gabriel Capone. Al Capone's reputation grew to make him the most infamous criminal in the United States. His name is still synonymous with the Chicago underworld. F.B.I. Collections.*

he was cocky, young, good looking, flashy and loved to be in the spotlight. In 1927, he was picked up by police on a misdemeanor charge. As the police were taking him to be arraigned, one of the cops, tired of Drucci's constant berating of the police and probably on the Capone payroll, shot him several times while he sat in the back of the police car.

Drucci's death led to the hard hitting George "Bugs" Moran ascending to the head of the gang. Moran had a deep hatred of Al Capone and vowed to see him dead.

In revenge, the North Siders gunned down some South Side men and Al "Scarface" Capone was determined to avenge the murders.

A scheme was concocted to lure "Bugs" Moran and some of his henchmen to a warehouse where the North Side gang stored whiskey.

One of Capone's men got someone close to Moran to tell him that a shipment of hijacked whiskey would be delivered to the warehouse on the morning of February 14, and that Moran should be there.

Seven of Moran's men waited in the warehouse for the delivery. Moran was late in getting there and just as he was driving up, he saw a police car pull up to the warehouse. He drove on by and stopped down the block for a coffee, waiting for the police to leave.

Two uniformed cops and three plain clothes men walked into the warehouse. A short time later the repeated blasts of "Tommy Guns" rang out shattering the silence of the cold February morning.

When the real police arrived they found that Moran's men had been lined up along the wall and machine gunned down. The blood ran thick on the floor of the warehouse. Seven men had mercilessly been shot, some almost cut in half by the high powered Thompson sub machine guns.

Six of the seven men killed in the massacre were hoodlums with thick files at the Chicago Police station; one was a man without a criminal record.

The men who were killed in the warehouse were:

Dr. Reinhart H. Schwimmer: an optometrist who enjoyed associating with the gangster element. He was known to brag about his gangster friends. Dr. Schwimmer and his curiosity about the gangster life took him to the wrong place that night.

Peter Gusenberg: a character with a twenty-seven year history of crime and a leader in the Moran gang. He served time in Joliet Prison on burglary charges and was later sent to Leavenworth for robbery.

Frank Gusenberg: Brother to Peter, and a man with a violent past having served several jail and prison sentences.

Albert R. Weishank: Owner of the Alcazar Club and official of the Central Cleaners and Dyers company. The police theorized he had joined the gang just months earlier when Moran tried to take over the leadership of the cleaning and dying industry in Chicago.

James Clark: A brother-in-law to "Bugs" Moran and a career criminal having served four jail sentences for robbery and burglary.

John May: A known safecracker with a jail record who worked for the North Side Gang.

Adam Heyer: A criminal with four visits to jail for robbery and running a confidence game and owner of the S. M. C. Cartiledge Company where the murders took place.

*A young Prohibition Agent, Eliot Ness, was appointed as a special agent to put an end to the bloodshed and tyranny of Al Capone. Photograph from the FBI Collections.*

The February 14th attack on the seven men in a "Bugs" Moran liquor warehouse became known as the "St. Valentine's Day Massacre." The results of the massacre backfired on Al Capone. His power seemed to dim after the highly publicized killings. Chicagoans were disgusted with the brutality of the killings and the tide began to switch from protecting and respecting the gangsters to a desire by the public for peace and safety on the streets.

The federal government also was fed up with the wholesale murder and lawlessness of Chicago that spread its tentacles across the nation. The new President, Herbert Hoover, was determined

to rid the nation of the scourge of hoodlums who held some of the country's greatest cities hostage. Hoover assigned U.S. District Attorney George E. Johnson to investigate and put an end to Al Capone's violations of the Volstead Act.

# The Intelligent Murderers - Leopold And Leob

The wealthy are not automatically excluded from crime because of their money or social standing. In 1924, a crime involving some of Chicago's wealthiest and most prominent families was splashed across the headlines of newspapers around the county.

The 14-year-old son of an affluent Chicago area businessman was kidnapped and killed and the men who committed the crime were also born into wealth and lived in the same elite neighborhood.

On May 21,1924, 14-year-old Bobby Franks disappeared while walking home from school. Bobby was the son of Jacob and Flora Franks who lived in the prosperous neighborhood of Kenwood in Chicago, Illinois. Mr. Franks started his business empire with a pawnshop and parlayed his income into real estate holdings worth millions.

Jacob and Flora Franks were upset with Bobby for not coming right home from school, thinking Bobby had gone to a friend's house. As the afternoon grew to evening and Bobby had still not returned home, the Franks became concerned.

Mrs. Franks began to call Bobby's friend's homes and Mr. Franks contacted the Headmaster of the Harvard School, the private school where Bobby was a student. He told the Headmaster that Bobby had not returned home from school and inquired if he could have somehow been locked in at the school.

Mr. Franks, a friend and the Headmaster searched the entire school building but Bobby was not to be found.

Chicago ---

Illinois

While the men were searching the school, Mrs. Franks received a telephone call from someone named Mr. Johnson. Mr. Johnson curtly said, "Your son has been kidnapped. He is all right. There will be further news in the morning." Mrs. Franks fainted in shock.

Mr. Franks and his attorney friend went to the police, but due to the lateness of the hour, none of the officers the attorney could trust were available. They decided to wait until morning.

The frantic parents waited impatiently for the telephone to ring with news of their son. Instead the kidnapper contacted them through a special delivery letter:

*Dear Sir:*

> *As you no doubt know at this time. Your son has been kidnapped. Allow us to assure you that he is at present well and safe. You need fear no physical harm for him, provided you live up carefully to the following instructions and to such others as you will receive by future communications. Should you, however, disobey any of the instructions, even slightly, his death will be the penalty.*

> *For obvious reasons make absolutely no attempt to communicate with either police authorities or any private agency. Should you already have communicated with the*

*14-year-old Bobby Franks*

*police, let them continue with their investigation, but do not mention this letter.*

*Secure before noon today $10,000.00. This money must be composed entirely of old bills of the following denominations: $2,000.00 in $20.00 bills, $8,000.00 in $50.00 bills. The money must be old. Any attempt to include new or marked bills will render the entire venture futile.*

*The money should be placed in a large cigar box, or if this is impossible, in a heavy cardboard box, securely closed and wrapped in white paper. The wrapping paper should be sealed at all openings with sealing wax.*

*Have the money with you, prepared as directed above, and remain at home after one o'clock. See that the telephone is not in use.*

*You will receive a future communication instructing you as to your future course.*

*As a final word of warning - this is a strictly commercial proposition, and we are prepared to put our threat into execution should we have reason to believe that you committed an infraction of the above instructions. However, should you carefully follow out our instructions to the letter, we can assure you that your son will be returned to you safely within six hours of our receipt of the money.*

*Yours truly,*
*George Johnson*

Mr. Franks immediately left the house to gather the money in the denominations the kidnapper requested, while his lawyer friend went to the police to report the crime and the receipt of the ransom letter.

*Loeb mansion in the Kentwood section of Chicago.*

Also living in the elite neighborhood of Kenwood on Chicago's south side were two very intelligent young men, both children of extremely wealthy parents. The men, Richard Loeb, 18-years-old and 19-year-old Nathan Leopold, had servants to wait on them, chauffeurs at their disposal, and private tennis courts and swimming pools on the grounds of their sprawling mansions.

Richard Loeb was born in June of 1905 to Anna and Albert Loeb. Mr. Loeb was an accomplished attorney before becoming the Vice President of Sears and Roebuck Company. The couple lived in Kenwood but also had a plush summer estate in Charlevoix, Michigan.

Nathan Leopold was born in November, 1904, the second son of a wealthy manufacturer. His father pampered and spoiled Nathan and his siblings after their mother died. The children were raised by a series of governesses; some were strict, teaching the children discipline and self-control, while others challenged the children's intellect.

*Nathan Leopold's home in Kenwood.*

Leopold thrived intellectually and excelled at school yet he was small in stature with below average looks. He graduated from his private secondary school, the Harvard School, and enrolled at the University of Chicago at age 15.

Loeb, in comparison to Leopold, was handsome, well liked and athletic, and with his exceptional intelligence was admitted to the University of Chicago as a freshman at the age of 13. It was while the two attended college that Loeb became fast friends with Leopold, a relationship that would go beyond simple male companionship.

Entering college at such an early age reinforced both Leopold and Loeb's arrogant feelings. They knew through their academic and

*Nathan Leopold, age 19 and Richard Loeb age 18.*

intellectual accomplishments that they were superior to everyone they knew.

The next semester both boys transferred from the University of Chicago in Illinois to the University of Michigan in Ann Arbor, Michigan. Loeb graduated at the age of 17, the youngest in the University of Michigan's history. (Although records are not available to substantiate this claim.)

There are many terms that can be used to portray Nathan Leopold Jr. and Richard Albert Loeb: egotistical, and conceited, but the most descriptive term would be arrogant.

After returning to Chicago, the two began to plot a crime. They believed that their superior intellect would allow them to commit the perfect crime. They thought out every possible scenario; the crime to commit, the time to do it, the victim, how to mislead the police, how not to leave any clues which would point back to them. They were students of crime novels, they knew the mistakes others had made and how to avoid them. They felt they were smarter than the police.

Before Mr. Franks returned home with the money, $10,000.00 in the correct denominations in a box wrapped in white paper, the police called; a body of a young boy had been found.

A railroad crew working on tracks near Wolf Lake by Hammond, Indiana, discovered the body of a young boy under a small culvert. It was just by chance that the crew was working that section of track, and it was by chance one of them looked in the culvert.

The police called Mr. Franks with the information. Mr. Franks was devastated by the news although when he heard the description the police provided of the boy, Mr. Franks said it couldn't be his son. But just to make sure Mr. Franks' brother-in-law was sent to verify it was not Bobby.

The telephone in the Franks home rang; Jacob's attorney friend answered.

The voice on the line said:

"This is George Johnson. I am sending a Yellow Cab for you. Get in and go to the drugstore at 1465 East Sixty-Third Street."

The lawyer handed the telephone receiver to Mr. Franks. George Johnson repeated the message to Jacob.

Neither of the men, in the intensity of the situation, wrote down the address of the drugstore, nor could remember it. They wracked their minds trying to remember the four digits and to confuse matters more, the street name made up of numbers.

Without the address they could not follow the instructions given to them; they could not deliver the money. Bobby might pay the ultimate penalty for their error.

As they thought about the address, the telephone rang again. Hoping it was George Johnson calling again they gathered a pen and paper to record the address.

It was Jacob's brother-in-law calling from the police department. A Pennsylvania railroad crew had pulled a body from a culvert at Wolf Lake; it was indeed Bobby Franks.

Learning that his son was dead was like a kick in the stomach to Jacob. His worry over the forgotten drugstore address was no longer an urgent matter; his son had already been killed. Now he had to do

the hardest thing he would ever have to do; tell his wife their little boy was dead.

The Yellow Cab arrived at the Franks' house, but the driver was told only to pick up a passenger at the Franks' Kentwood address, not the destination. The cab could not help find the kidnappers/ killers.

The Chicago Police Department launched an intensive investigation into the death of the boy.

Police swarmed the area of the culvert where the body was found, although the railroad crew had disturbed the crime scene when they pulled the boy's body out. The boy's clothes and a pair of glasses were found nearby.

Other officers scrutinized the ransom letter that was delivered to the Franks' house. Through the perfect grammar and word selection, they surmised the kidnapper was a well-educated person, an intelligent person who would challenge the investigative skills of the police.

They also determined the letter was typed on a small Underwood portable typewriter. Due to the unevenness of the letter strike and other slight mistakes made with the typewriter, the police surmised the person who typed the letter was not a professional typist.

Based on these assumptions, the police focused their attention on three teachers at the Harvard School where Bobby Franks attended. The teachers were taken into custody and their homes searched. The men were questioned at length but in the end all were released.

The police discovered that the glasses found near the body did not belong to the boy or any of the railroad crew.

The glasses were of a common prescription and a common design, and photographs of the glasses in the newspapers did not bring about any credible leads. The police took the eyeglasses to area optometrists and optical companies. They discovered the hinges on the glasses were

*The glasses found at the railroad culvert.*

very unusual; in fact, they were sold through only one optometrist and he had sold only three sets of glasses with the unique hinges.

Now they questioned whether the glasses had anything to do with the murder. Were they evidence directly from the murder of the boy or were they simply glasses lost in the area?

The police visited each person to determine if they had anything to do with the crime.

One pair of the eyeglasses with the unusual hinges had been sold to a neighbor of the dead boy, Nathan Leopold.

Police visited the Leopold house. It was a sprawling mansion belonging to one of the wealthiest, influential and socially connected men in Chicago.

The police showed Nathan the glasses and asked if they were his. Nathan claimed they weren't, stating his were in his room. When asked to see his glasses, Nathan could not produce them. He told the police that he must have lost them. After more questioning he agreed that the glasses could be his.

When he asked where they had found them, he was told near Wolf Lake and questioned how his glasses came to be out in the isolated wooded area in Indiana.

Nathan readily answered that he was an avid ornithologist. In fact he was a recognized expert, he had even written a book on the subject. He told them that he often taught classes on bird identification in the Wolf

Lake area. When he was last there he had tripped and the glasses must have fallen from his breast pocket.

The police asked him to re-enact the trip with the glasses in his breast pocket and each time the glasses did not fall from the pocket.

When asked where he was the evening of May 21, 1924, the night Bobby Franks was murdered, he responded that he and a friend, Richard Loeb, had gone birding and then picked up some girls, although he didn't know the girls' last names.

The police were suspicious of Nathan Leopold. The Illinois State Attorney, Robert Crowe, was put in charge of the investigation and decided they needed to further question Nathan and his alibi Loeb.

Being a politician, Crowe was hesitant to pull the sons of two of Chicago's most influential residents into the police station for questioning. Newspaper reporters had swarmed the station since the body of Bobby Franks was found. Camera flashes would capture the boys entering the station and the papers would have them tried and convicted before their questioning had begun. To maintain decorum, protect the rights of the two boys and not to do anything to alienate the wealthy population of the city, State Attorney Crowe, a man with political aspirations, had Leopold and Loeb taken to the LaSalle Hotel.

Loeb and Leopold were kept apart so they could not discuss their alibis, delivered in separate vehicles and interviewed in separate rooms. In fact, neither knew the other was being questioned.

The homes of the two were searched while they were being questioned. The police found letters at Leopold's house that depicted homosexual acts; they also found study notes Leopold had typed.

When confronted with what the police found at his house, he explained that he was going to translate an Italian journal that contained the sexually explicit material. He adamantly denied having a sexual relationship with Loeb. But when they presented the typed notes that were typed on the same typewriter the ransom note had been typed on, he said he had used a portable typewriter a couple of times but it wasn't his; it belonged to someone else.

Both Leopold and Loeb said they were driving Leopold's car on the night in question. They claimed they had driven Leopold's car to go birding and they also used the car to meet the girls and drive around with them. But when the Leopold family chauffeur was questioned, he said Nathan's car was in the garage all day. He knew it had not left the garage because Nathan had complained about the brakes squeaking and the chauffeur had worked on them that day.

When the police informed Loeb that they had caught them in a lie about the car, he knew they had been caught. He asked to talk to States' Attorney Crowe.

Over the next few hours both Leopold and Loeb told how they had conspired to commit the perfect crime.

The two intelligent teenage boys told how they had spent months planning and perfecting the crime. They didn't do it for the money; they did it as an experiment to prove they could do it. They worked and re-worked the plan. They approached the kidnapping as if it were a complex mathematical equation; if we do this... then this will happen... but what if this happens... then we will have to do this...

They had not pre-selected a victim, rather they determined criteria by which to select a victim. It had to be a boy, he had to be from affluent parents, he had to be someone one of them knew so they could easily stop and talk to the boy and get him to get into the car without causing a scene. They coldly, without discussion, agreed that the victim would have to be killed so he wouldn't identify them.

They found the collecting of the ransom to be the most challenging part of the project. They came up with money transfer scenarios then analyzed them, picking them apart until they thought they had perfected it.

They theorized that most kidnapping suspects were caught while the ransom money was being transferred. They would minimize their risk through an elaborate scheme. They would have a cab pick up the victim's father and take him to a destination near a train station. He would be told to board a train and sit in a specific location and when the train passed a landmark he was to toss the money from the train. Then Leopold and Loeb could pick up the money undetected.

Dear Sir:

Proceed immediately to the back platform of the train. Watch the east side of the track. Have your package ready. Look for the first LARGE, RED, BRICK factory situated immediately adjoining the tracks on the east. On top of this factory is a large, black watertower with the word CHAMPION written on it. Wait until you have COMPLETELY passed the south end of the factory - count five very rapidly and then IMMEDIATELY throw the package as far east as you can.

Remember that this is your only chance to recover your son.

Yours truly,

GEORGE JOHNSON

*The second ransom note that was to be delivered to Mr. Franks*

On May 1, 1924, they put their plan for the perfect crime into action.

Knowing the car used to pick up their victim might be seen and identified, they rented a car using a false name to use in the kidnapping. Since he wouldn't be using his car that day, Leopold arranged for his chauffeur to check into the squeaking brakes, a decision that ultimately led to his being caught.

Leopold and Loeb drove the streets near the Harvard School at the end of the school day looking for a victim. They noticed Bobby Franks walking home just two blocks from his house.

Richard knew Bobby because they were neighbors. Bobby often went to the Loeb house to play tennis. He would make the perfect victim; someone they knew and his father was a millionaire.

The car slowed and Richard asked Bobby if he wanted a ride home, but since he was just a few blocks from home he refused the offer.

Richard then tried to lure Bobby to the car by asking him about a tennis racket he had used at the Loeb tennis court. Bobby approached and entered the car, getting in the front seat. As Leopold drove off, Loeb put his left hand over Bobby's mouth and began to beat the boy's head with the wood handle of a chisel. Bobby's death did not come as quickly as they had anticipated, so a sock was stuffed down the boy's throat. The sock choked the boy and Bobby died of suffocation in minutes.

The car, with the dead body covered in a blanket, and the killers drove the ten miles to Wolf Lake. The callous murderers were pleased with the success of their crime so far. It had worked to perfection, just like they had planned. They even stopped en-route for a celebration sandwich at a roadside hot dog stand. They had no remorse. They were superior.

The killers drove to the Wolf Lake area and stripped the boy of his clothes. So as to deter easy identification of Bobby's body, acid was pored on his face and penis. They had a thought that the penis was as individual as fingerprints and a means of identification. Then they stuffed the body beneath the railroad culvert. They thought the body was well hidden and would not be discovered for weeks, well after Loeb and Leopold had received their ransom.

On the way back, they placed the first call to Jacob Franks, telling him his son had been kidnapped.

Back in Kentwood, they burned the bloodstained clothes they had worn, cleaned bloodstains from the rented car, and discarded the chisel. The next morning they mailed the special delivery letter to Mr. and Mrs. Franks and made a second call to the Franks' residence, telling him the address of the drugstore where he would receive his next instructions.

*Nathan Leopold, Clarence Darrow and Richard Loeb. From the Author's Collection.*

The confessions were followed by a lengthy trial, the "Trial of the Century" as it became known. Newspapers from across the country ran daily articles reporting who the witnesses were and what they said.

The well-known attorney, Clarence Darrow, represented both Leopold and Loeb. He was hired for his strong stand against capital punishment. Nathan and Richard were guilty; they both admitted it, but the Loeb family hired Darrow to keep the boys from hanging for their crime.

Darrow knew that if the trial went to a jury, the viciousness of the crime would result in the jury handing down a death penalty. To avoid a jury trial, Darrow pleaded both Richard and Nathan guilty. The question of whether they had committed the crime was not the issue. The issue became whether they should be hung for their crime and Judge John R. Caverly would make that decision at a sentencing hearing.

For defense attorney Clarence Darrow, the main focus of the trial was not the men's guilt, not if they should live or die, but rather used the case to expound on the legality and morality of capital punishment.

Almost four months after 14-year-old Bobby Franks was killed by Richard Loeb and Nathan Leopold, Judge Cavely sentenced both Loeb and Leopold to life in prison, plus ninety-nine years.

As he announced his decision, the judge was very clear he was not doing the boys any favors by sparing their lives. He said; "To the offenders, particularly of the type they are, the prolonged years of confinement may well be the severest form of retribution."

# The Intelligent Murderers

Both Loeb and Leopold were housed in the Illinois Correctional Institution at Joliet, Illinois, where they were to serve the sentence for the death of Bobby Franks.

When they first were sent to Joliet, authorities tried to keep the two apart but it didn't last for long. Within a few years Richard and Nathan had started a school for inmates and were together as they administrated and taught at the school.

On January 28, 1936, after serving less than twelve years of his sentence, another inmate killed Richard Loeb. Loeb was slashed 58 times with a straight razor. The inmate who killed Loeb claimed he was only fighting off Loeb's sexual advances. The inmate was tried and acquitted of the charges, for Loeb's homosexual promiscuity was well known throughout the prison.

Leopold remained in prison until 1958 when he was granted parole. He promptly moved to Puerto Rico and lived there until his death in 1971.

The perfectly planned crime had failed because of a number of blunders by the two intellectually superior criminals: Nathan Leopold's glasses had fallen out of his pocket when they dumped the body, having the chauffeur fix the brakes on Nathan's car proved the two had not used the car on the day of the murder as they claimed, and Bobby Franks' body, thought to be hidden in a perfect place, was found before the ransom was collected.

The "Crime of the Century" and the "Trial of the Century" resulted from nothing more than two bored and spoiled rich boys seeking a thrill. The ransom money was not their goal, it was simply an experiment by two arrogant teenagers. Their arrogance prevented them from feeling remorse and the pain of the Franks family at the loss of their son. The two psychopaths only wanted to satisfy their own selfish demented desires.

# Death By Hanging - William Williams

Love can make people think strangely, act strangely and make them do strange things. In 1905, one Minnesota man became so smitten by love that it led to his horrific, painful death.

William Williams immigrated to the United States from St. Ives, Cornwall in England at twenty years of age. He settled in Minnesota and drifted from job to job working as a miner and steam pipe fitter.

Williams was also a man known to have been in trouble with the authorities. By the time he was twenty seven, Bill Williams had deserted the British Army and served prison time for being an instigator of the mutiny of the Fifteenth Minnesota Volunteers while stationed in Georgia. He also served jail time for shooting another man in the arm during a barroom fight in Hibbing, Minnesota. The uneducated man had a violent personality.

In 1904, Bill Williams contracted diphtheria, a disease that was quite common in the early 1900s. It begins with a sore throat and low fever then progresses to an inflammation of the upper respiratory track. Today a case of diphtheria is extremely rare, but it one time accounted for 15,000 to 20,000 deaths per year.

While Bill Williams was in the hospital, he shared a room with Johnny Keller. The two were quarantined and spent a lot of time together. The 27-year-old Williams and the 15-year-old Johnny became fast friends; close intimate friends.

After their release from the hospital, over the objections of Johnny's parents, Bill and Johnny moved into an apartment in St. Paul. The man and boy also took extended trips to Winnipeg, Manitoba, Canada.

# Great Lakes Serial Killers

Johnny's father convinced the boy that the relationship he had with the older man was not healthy and the boy returned to his parent's house in St. Paul.

Williams was at a loss without his young lover and wrote letters to Johnny, some expressing his love, others threatening Johnny and his parents.

On the night of April 13, 1905, Bill Williams went to the Keller apartment to plead with Johnny's parents to allow the boy to live with him. Mr. Keller wasn't home, and since it was late and Johnny was already in bed, Bill made his case to Mrs. Keller.

During the conversation, Bill flew into rage, pulled a gun and shot Mrs. Keller. He then went to Johnny's bedroom where the boy was sleeping, took aim and shot twice, hitting the boy in the neck and the head. The boy died instantly.

William Williams had killed Johnny Keller, the object of his affections. At 1:00 am as he left the Keller's Reid Court apartment in a emotional state, he knocked on the door of another apartment and told the lady who answered to go the Keller apartment; they had been shot.

The murderer walked to the St. Paul Police station and told the police officer behind the desk that he had just shot two people and asked the officer to send a doctor to the Keller residence.

Williams was promptly taken into custody and later charged with the murder of Johnny Keller. Eight days after the attack Mrs. Keller died of her wounds.

At his trial, William Williams claimed a defense that he was in a state of emotional insanity when the crime occurred and he therefore should

SHOOTS MOTHER AND SON

DOUBLE TRAGEDY AT ST. PAUL
APPARENTLY THE DEED OF
A DEGENERATE.

not be put to death. The jury disagreed and sentenced him to die by hanging for the premeditated murder of Johnny Keller and his mother.

The case was appealed to the Minnesota Supreme Court, but they agreed with the verdict and upheld the sentence of death.

Williams was held in the Ramsey County jail on the first floor. He could hear men working on the gallows that was one floor beneath him in the basement. He heard nails pounded as the scaffold was built and he could hear when Sheriff Miesen tested the trap door Williams would soon fall through.

On the appointed day, February 13, 1906, William Williams walked from his jail cell with the Sheriff, the Reverend Cushen and a guard. The group descended the stairs to the basement where the gallows had been built. The Rev. Cushen put his arm around the shoulder of the condemned man as they walked, trying to ease the pain he must be experiencing.

Williams did not protest, did not balk; he walked straight towards the stairway to the top of the gallows. He climbed the stairs and stood on the platform of the wood scaffold.

The rope noose was placed over his head and adjusted snuggly around his neck. Sheriff Miesen asked Williams if he had anything to say before the sentence was carried out.

In a strong voice, Bill Williams said; *"Gentlemen, you are witnessing an illegal hanging. I am accused of killing Johnny Keller. He is the best friend I ever had."*

Rev. Cushen said a prayer and the hood was pulled down over Williams' head. The reverend stepped back and Sheriff Miesen pulled the lever opening the trapdoor.

William Williams fell feet first through the trapdoor.

Death by hanging is the result of one or more causes. The sudden stop as the victim falls and the rope becomes taut and separates the spinal cord causing the condemned to die instantly. Another cause in a hanging death occurs as the noose tightens around the neck compressing the windpipe causing death by strangulation. The third method of death is the result of the tight noose restricting the blood flow and starving the brain of life-giving blood.

The few witnesses present expected Williams' body to fall through the

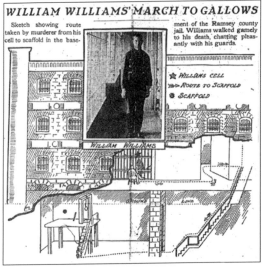

WILLIAM WILLIAMS' MARCH TO GALLOWS

Sketch showing route taken by murderer from his cell to scaffold in the basement of the Ramsey county jail. Williams walked gamely to his death, chatting pleasantly with his guards.

☆ WILLIAMS CELL
➤ ROUTE TO SCAFFOLD
● SCAFFOLD

WILLIAM WILLIAMS

GROUND LINE

platform of the gallows, the rope growing taut jerking his falling body to a stop.

In the hanging of William Williams for the deaths of Johnny Keller and his mother, Williams' body fell through the trapdoor as the rope pulled tight around his neck and the rope stretched allowing Williams to fall until his feet were resting on the floor. He was still alive.

The sheriff ordered three of his deputies to the top of the gallows to pull on the rope. The three men pulled on the rope raising Williams' body off the floor. A doctor in attendance, checking for vital signs indicated the condemned man was still alive. The deputies took turns holding the rope suspending Williams' body off the floor for fourteen and half minutes until the doctor pronounced him dead.

When Sheriff Miesen tested the gallows he did not correctly estimate the length of rope needed, the stretch of the rope, and the weight of the condemned.

There were few witnesses to the Williams execution and word of the atrocity was kept quiet until the *Pioneer Press* heard about it and printed an eyewitness report.

The citizenry of Minnesota were in an uproar. The newspapers asked how could such a barbaric thing happen. In 1911, when the topic of whether the Minnesota legislature should abolish capital punishment, the horrible death of William Williams was the deciding factor.

William Williams, the murderer of Johnny and Mrs. Keller and a man who died a slow, painful and prolonged death was the last person to be executed in Minnesota.

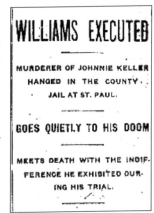

**WILLIAMS EXECUTED**

MURDERER OF JOHNNIE KELLER
HANGED IN THE COUNTY
JAIL AT ST. PAUL.

**GOES QUIETLY TO HIS DOOM**

MEETS DEATH WITH THE INDIF-
FERENCE HE EXHIBITED DUR-
ING HIS TRIAL.

# The Homicidal
# H. H. Holmes

Cities from around the Unites States were vying for the opportunity to host the 1893 World's Columbian Exposition, a celebration commemorating the 400th anniversary of the first landfall of Christopher Columbus on American soil.

New York City was the favored contender, but the eastern high finance tycoons were shocked when the exposition was awarded to the city of Chicago. They considered Chicago to be a dirty industrial city with several steel mills, the railroad hub of the Midwest and the nation's slaughterhouse and meatpacking center. Furthermore, since seventy percent of the population of the city were foreign born residents, the city was not thought of by the New York financiers to be cultured enough to host such an event.

Being selected to host the event was a boom to Chicago. The exposition would bring in visitors from around the world. They saw the exposition as an opportunity to show the world what made Chicago great.

The possibility of millions of people visiting Chicago was not lost on the criminal element. They saw this as an opportunity to make an illegal buck off the tourists. Along with the glitter and lights of the World's Columbian Exposition came the dark and sinister criminals.

The Chicago police would be kept busy with pickpockets, prostitutes, thugs, burglars and con men who flocked to Chicago to prey on the unsuspecting fair goers.

Along with the criminals out to make a buck from the millions who would visit Chicago during the exposition, many Chicago residents also

saw an opportunity to make money off the estimated 27 million who would venture to the city. Fruit and sandwich stands lined the streets near the fair grounds, any room available was put up for rent and restaurants seemed to open over night.

One enterprising Chicago pharmacist, H. H. Holmes, constructed a 100 room, three story motel in anticipation of the crowds the exposition would attract. The motel with its turrets and brick facade was referred to as "The Castle."

The Castle was close to the exposition site and advertised that the motel was just a short distance from the fairgrounds making it a safe place to stay for single young ladies in town to see the World's Columbian Exposition. The motel only catered to women, and many of them selected the" Castle" because they felt safe there.

**THE WORLD'S FAIR.**

———

**Opened by President Cleveland in Presence of a Multitude.**

———

**People from All Lands Participate in the Exercises—The Greatest Event in the History of Chicago.**

———

Born in 1861, Herman Webster Mudgett, later changed to Doctor Herman Henry Holmes, grew up in the town of Gilmanton Academy, New Hampshire. According to Mudgett, he attended the medical

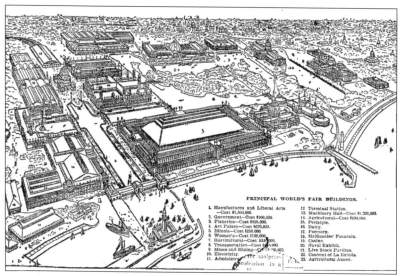

*An artist's rendition of the 1893 Columbian Exposition grounds.*

school at the University of Michigan and graduated as a physician, although records of a Herman Webster Mudgett attending the University of Michigan have not been found.

Not letting a medical degree stand in his way, Mudgett practiced medicine until he was found guilty of helping a patient fake his death by providing a cadaver and a death certificate. The purpose of this charade was to defraud an insurance company.

For a while he found employment as a physician in a hospital for the insane. He did not find this to his liking and moved on to another city.

Going by the name H.H. Holmes, he moved to Chicago.

Holmes found employment as a pharmacist's prescription clerk. Perhaps he was able to convince the pharmacist, Mrs. E. S. Holton, of his credentials because he had experience pretending to be a doctor.

Before long, Mrs. Holton and her daughter mysteriously moved to California and left the store and all it's inventory to H. H. Holmes.

Friends and neighbors of the Holton's thought it was suspicious, but when they inquired of their whereabouts the new owner told them that the ladies had a desire to move west.

The pharmacy was very successful and before long Holmes had enough money to purchase the land across the street to build his castle-like motel.

*The Castle, Holmes' motel which catered to young women visiting the World's Columbian Exposition. From the Author's Collection.*

The Castle Motel was a beautiful building and to the neighbors, a welcomed addition to the area. Those who stayed at the motel were not a disruption and the motel never seemed to want for customers.

At the close of the exposition, H. H. Holmes' felt it was time for him to move on. Holmes purchased a substantial insurance policy on the building, fortunately for him, just before it caught fire and was damaged. With the large insurance policy and fire of unknown origin, arson was suspected, and the pharmacist vanished.

Landing in Philadelphia, Pennsylvania in 1894, Holmes was in need of money. He joined with two other men to scam an insurance company in another fake death scheme. Holmes obtained a medical school cadaver, placed it in a laboratory, and started a fire. The body was supposed to be that of one of his partners, Benjamin Pitezel.

The body was so damaged from chemical burns to the face and the resulting fire that H. H. Holmes and a 15-year-old daughter of Pitezel's could only identify the body as being Pitezel from recognizable marks on unburned portions of the corpse.

The $10,000.00 insurance policy on Mr. Pitezel was paid out with Pitezel's wife, Carrie, being the beneficiary. Holmes went with her and collected the money and before it was divided with the other criminals, Holmes left town taking the money and the Pitezel's three children with him.

Holmes had disappeared with the money, and one of his criminal accomplices, angry that he had been cheated out of his share of the money, went to the police and told the whole story.

He told the authorities that a cadaver was going to be used but rather Holmes had killed Benjamin Pitezel and planted his body in the laboratory.

The insurance company hired the Pinkerton Detective Agency to find the man who defrauded them out of the money.

*Herman Webster Mudgett, who later changed to Doctor Herman Henry Holmes. From the Author's Collection.*

Frank Geyer was assigned as the lead detective on the case. Geyer was given letters the children had written to their mother and the detective was able to track Holmes and the children from Philadelphia to Cincinnati, Ohio, to Indianapolis, Indiana, to Chicago, Illinois, to Detroit, Michigan and finally to Toronto, Canada.

The detective finally caught up with Holmes in Vermont. The local police were made aware of the suspect and put him under surveillance. When Holmes traveled to Boston to board a ship for Europe, he was arrested and taken back to Philadelphia.

The children of Benjamin Pitezel unfortunately met the same fate at the hands of Holmes as their father had. The burned remains of 8-year-old Howard were found in the ash pan of a stove in a house in Indianapolis. The detectives learned that Holmes had rented the house. The bodies of the two girls, Alice, 15-year-old, and Nellie, 11-year-old, were found buried in the basement of a house Holmes had rented in Toronto. The girls' remains were so putrefied that they were only identified by the children's hair, clothing and teeth.

NELLIE PIETZEL.

The death of the three children and their father made headlines across the country. In Chicago, the authorities took another look at the "Castle" that Holmes had owned.

What they found at the Castle made even the most veteran of the Chicago cops shutter. The building was a virtual torture chamber.

The motel was built so that Holmes could freely move about through secret passageways and observe his guests through peepholes. There were gas pipes leading into certain rooms that were controlled by Holmes. With a flip of a valve he could asphyxiate a woman and enjoy watching through the peephole as she choked to death.

There is evidence that sometimes Holmes would open the valve, filling a specially designed asbestos lined room with gas and then he would ignite it so he could watch the poor woman burn to death.

HOWARD PIETZEL.

Once a woman was killed in her room, Holmes could open a trap door and send her body down a chute to the basement where her corpse was disposed of.

ALICE PIETZEL.

He might put the corpse into one of two very large furnaces to be burned to ashes. He sometimes stripped the body of flesh and boiled the bones clean. Or he could soak the body in a vat of acid to decay the flesh and soften the bones.

In his house of horrors, Holmes had a room equipped for surgery and a hangman's noose. The noose was found to have the residue of human blood; it had been used. He also had a room equipped with devices to torture the women. One device was a bed with straps to hold the living young woman while Holmes turned a wheel causing the bed to separate and stretch the young woman until she was literally torn apart.

Holmes did not burn the bodies of all of his victims; he sometimes soaked their bodies in large vats of acid to melt the flesh from the bones. The acid bath and boiling of the corpses accounted for the many complete skeletons the police found hidden in the Castle. Holmes was

A STUDY OF HOLMES FROM LIFE.
Sketched in the courtroom by Homer Davenport.

suspected of selling the skeletons to medical students as study tools. He also sold organs he had removed from the young women to medical schools.

From prison in Philadelphia, Holmes claimed the horror stories coming out of Chicago were nothing more than sensationalized journalism to guarantee that he would not receive a fair trial and be found guilty of murdering Benjamin Pitezel. He adamantly said he was innocent of all the crimes of which he was being accused.

When he realized no one was buying his story, Holmes decided to write his memoirs to clear his reputation. He wrote that the only crime he participated in was helping a woman who worked for him dispose of the body of the woman's sister. He said she had killed her own sister in a fit of jealousy because the sister had paid too much attention to Holmes. Again no one believed his story.

A jury found H. H. Holmes guilty and a judge sentenced him to death by hanging.

Sitting in jail while appeals were being filed on his behalf, Holmes presented a third story. This time he claimed to have killed more than 100 people. He determined if he was guilty he might as well be the most notorious killer in the United States, but he changed the story again claiming he had only killed 27 people.

On May 7, 1896, H. H. Holmes was sent to the gallows and hung for the murder of Benjamin Pitezel.

# HOLMES IS HANGED,

### The Multi-Murderer Has Paid the Last Penalty.

## NERVY TO THE LAST.

He Declared His Innocence as He
Stood Upon the
Scaffold.

## PRIESTS IN ATTENDANCE.

The Doomed Man Prayed Fervently 'Ere
They Adjusted the
Noose.

## A SHORT DRAMATIC SPEECH.

He Slept Soundly During the Night an
Ate a Very Hearty
Breakfast.

Holmes was sentenced to death for the one murder, admitted to only assisting in disposing of a body, then admitted to killing over 100, then he admitted to murdering only 27 people, but the authorities have conservatively estimated that Holmes may be responsible for as many as 150 deaths. Many of the murders occurred in Holmes "Motel of Death," where young women checked in but did not check out.

# The Vicious Rapes And Murders Of Bernardo And Homolka

The young pretty woman was jogging on a sidewalk in Scarborough, Ontario, as she had done many evenings. Nothing was out of the ordinary as she ran, ear plugs in, music playing, in her Spandex running shorts and top. She was deep in her own thoughts. She wasn't aware of the man following her.

The man, in his early twenties, quickened his pace, came up behind her, covered her mouth with one hand while he roughly pulled her behind the bushes. The rapist ripped the clothes from the terrified young woman and forced her to perform fellatio on him then he vaginally raped her.

The rapes, which began in May of 1987, were not always so violent; at first he only sexually groped his victims. He progressed to roughly undressing women and forcefully inserting his fingers into them. Each attack became more vicious.

The man known as the Scarborough Rapist preyed on young women, sneaking up on them from behind, taking them by surprise, and throwing them to the ground. The attacks grew more violent, until he sadistically forced the women to endure painful forced anal sex, and demanded fellatio all the while he talked to her throughout the ordeal. He took great pleasure in humiliating the women.

The police investigated the rapes and determined, through the evidence that they were probably dealing with one individual, a serial rapist.

The victims were able to provide some description of the assailant; the man was young, well-groomed, good teeth, and "did not" have a bad odor. Not enough for the police to find the rapist.

By 1988 the police were investigating eleven rapes they suspected were all done by the same person. The victims collaborated in producing a composite sketch of the man who had raped them.

When the composite sketch was released to the public, the police received several hundred leads. Several of them lead them to Paul Bernardo, the man who would ultimately be arrested for the series of rapes which earned him the title, "The Scarborough rapist."

In October of 1987, Paul Bernardo met a pretty 17-year-old girl in a restaurant in Scarborough. When Paul Bernardo met Karla Homolka the result was the same as it is when gas is thrown on a fire. The couple were hot, passionate, and uncontrollable.

Karla was living in St. Catherine's, Ontario, and working at a pet store. She and a friend were in Scarborough attending a conference for their employer. She was pretty, vivacious, and her sexuality was obvious. Paul was instantly attracted to Karla.

Paul was twenty three-years-old, blond and good-looking and employed by Price Waterhouse as a junior accountant. He was nothing like the other guys Karla had dated. They were just boys and Paul was a professional in the business world. Karla was instantly attracted to Paul.

That night Karla and her girlfriend and Paul and his friend went to the girls' motel room for drinks. In just over two hours after Paul and Karla met they were making hot passionate love in the bed while the other couple was also in the room.

This was the beginning of the relationship between two of Canada's most notorious murderers.

The 70 plus miles separating Paul in Scarborough, an eastern section of Toronto, and Karla's home of St. Catherine's, on the Canadian side of the Niagara River didn't keep the two apart. He made weekend trips to visit her and her family, and by December 1989 the couple was engaged.

In 1990 there were many changes for the young couple; Paul lost his job as an accountant with Price Waterhouse and began smuggling cigarettes into Canada from the United States, Karla quit her job at the pet store and took a job working for a veterinarian, and the Metro Toronto Police in connection with their Scarborough rapist investigation questioned Paul.

*The police sketch of the Scarborough Rapist.*

He willingly provided hair, blood and saliva samples and joked with the detectives about how much he himself thought he resembled the composition drawing, but nothing came of it.

Karla was so much in love with Paul, she would do anything for him. She gladly submitted to Paul's sometime painful and perverse sexual desires and was subservient to Paul's domineering personality. She was so afraid of losing Paul that if he wanted something, she would do it for him.

Despite their outward appearance as a beautiful, loving couple, Paul was angry that Karla had given herself to another man before they had met. He convinced Karla that since she was not a virgin when they met that it was her responsibility to provide him a virgin he could deflower. His choice was Karla's fifteen-year-old sister, Tammy.

They devised a plan where Karla could make her man happy by giving him her sister's virginity as a gift. On December 23, 1991, after a Homolka family Christmas party, Karla and Paul took Tammy into the basement while the rest of the family slept. The young girl was given drinks laced with sedatives Karla had stolen from the veterinarian's office.

Tammy passed out from the drinks and drugs. Tammy's jeans were removed and just as Paul began to enter the girl, Tammy started to vomit. In her drunk/drugged unconscious state the young girl began to choke on the vomit. Paul was disgusted with the events; it was not the beautiful sexual experience he had hoped for, when suddenly Tammy stopped breathing.

Karla and Paul tried to revive her but she wasn't breathing. Karla called the ambulance and hid the drugs while Paul dressed the girl. When the ambulance arrived they quickly took the unconscious girl to the hospital where she was pronounced dead.

The coroner determined the cause of death to be accidental asphyxiation from choking on her own vomit. A blood toxicology test was not made and the drugs in her system were not detected.

In a matter of weeks, the Scarborough rapist struck in St. Catherine's.

Paul picked up a hitchhiker and took her back to the Homolka house while Karla's parents were out. Paul raped the girl in Karla's bed.

Karla was home at the time. She knew what Paul was doing but she was so in love with Paul and so afraid if she protested that Paul would beat her or worse yet leave her, Karla said or did nothing.

The girl was lucky, Paul Bernado drove the frightened girl to a secluded area and let her go.

In Karla's mind she had let her man down. She had not provided him with a virgin so she set out to find another for him. She selected a fifteen-year-old friend of her sister's who actually resembled Tammy.

Karla invited the young girl to the house that she and Paul shared. The young girl was a friend of Karla's. The girl worshipped Karla. Karla was beautiful and Karla was everything she wanted to be. She eagerly accepted the invitation to spend time with Karla and her handsome fiance.

Using the same animal sedative she used on her sister, Karla laced the drinks she made for the young girl. Soon the girl had passed out and Karla called Paul to come for his gift.

Paul was overjoyed with the prospect that lay before him, a virgin who resembled Tammy, his for the taking.

Paul was concerned about the drug Karla had used after it had killed Tammy, but Karla convinced him that she knew what she was doing.

Paul videotaped Karla undressing the unconscious girl, and then at Paul's direction Karla made love to the girl. Paul then took the girl's virginity. Not satisfied, he turned the girl over and took her anally.

The next morning the girl awoke, sick to her stomach and sore. She was another of the lucky ones and she went home.

Karla invited the girl over on several occasions. Paul once kissed the girl in front of Karla, a long passionate kiss. She was horrified; she told Karla she didn't do anything to lure Paul. Karla told her it was okay, Paul liked her and she didn't mind Paul kissing her.

When the girl told Paul that she didn't like him and that she didn't want to see him again, Paul blew up, calling her all kinds of foul and degrading names. The relationship with the girl ended.

Paul and some friends were making a substantial amount of money smuggling American cigarettes into Canada where cigarettes were much more expensive. During the night, Paul would steal automobile license plates to cover his frequent trips across the border. At 2:00 am on June 14, 1991, he was in a neighborhood stealing plates when he found 14-year-old Leslie Mahaffy wandering around. Leslie, the pretty girl with long blond hair and braces on her teeth had been locked out of her house because she broke her curfew. Fed up with her daughter ignoring family rules, Mrs. Mahaffy decided to teach her daughter a lesson and she locked the doors. Leslie would either have to ring the bell to wake the family or remain outdoors till morning.

Had she not been outside waiting to get into her house that night, Paul Bernardo would not have been able to abduct the girl at knifepoint and force her into his car.

Paul took Leslie back to the house where he and Karla lived. While Karla slept, Paul set up his video camera and filmed the naked and blindfolded child. When Karla awoke and found that Paul had gotten a new plaything she was angry, but soon, at Paul's insistence, Karla joined in the debauchery.

He videotaped Karla making love to the child, then she held the camera as he violated Leslie. The horrible ordeal lasted over twenty-four hours. Towards the end, Paul and Karla had tied Leslie up in binder twine and Paul set the video camera to document him sodomizing the girl.

Paul and Karla discussed what they would do with Leslie now that they were through with her. A decision was made; they would drug her, dress her and drop her off near where Paul had picked her up. That way she couldn't tell anyone what had happened or identify Paul and Karla.

According to Paul, by the time they got around to moving her, Leslie was dead. Paul said at his trial that they theorized Leslie must have died from the combination of the drugs and the alcohol they had served her. But when Karla later testified against Paul, she said Paul had strangled Leslie with an electrical cord.

To dispose of the body, the couple took the corpse into the basement and, using a circular saw, Paul cut Leslie's body into small pieces.

The next day while Karla was at work, Paul made blocks with bags of cement that can be purchased at hardware stores. Within the cement blocks he embedded Leslie's body parts.

Paul took the blocks to Lake Gibson and threw them into the water.

Karla justified her involvement in the rape and murder and dismemberment of Leslie Mahaffy because her man wanted it and her sole purpose in life was to please her man.

On June 29, 1991, Karla and Paul were united in marriage. The ceremony was extravagant, complete with horse drawn white carriages and a sit down meal at an exclusive hall. Paul wanted to show the world he was successful and nothing but the best was good enough for him. What his wife wanted was irrelevant. After all, he did make sure their wedding vows include the phrase that Karla would "love, honor and obey" him.

Despite that fact that Karla would do anything Paul wanted to satisfy his every sexual fantasy, Paul wanted another girl… another virgin.

Ten months after their wedding Paul and Karla went out scouting for a girl, a young, virginal schoolgirl.

The couple drove the streets near schools as school was letting out. Paul noticed a girl walking by herself. He drove by her a couple of times to see if she interested him.

Paul pulled into the parking lot of a church where the girl would pass. Karla opened her window and called to the girl. Karla explained that they were lost and asked the girl for help. The young schoolgirl, Kristen French, readily walked to the car to help them.

Asking Kristen to show her the directions on a map, Karla got out of the passenger's seat and spread the map on the roof. While the girl looked at the map, Paul came around behind her and forced her into the car. Karla jumped in the back and grabbed the girl's hair holding her down while Paul got back behind the wheel.

When they arrived back at their house, Paul took Kristen up to the bedroom to have some fun with his new toy. When Karla joined them, she found Kristen sitting on the floor crying. They asked the girl questions trying to calm her. Kristen told them she was fifteen-years-old and was active in school activities.

The questions ended when Paul was ready for sex. The couple stripped Kristen of her clothes and Paul raped her. Then at Paul's direction Karla raped the girl.

Paul warned the girl not to complain and to do whatever was asked of her and she would be able to return home. But if she refused, Paul would close his fists and beat her. Kristen was scared but compliant.

Paul told her that she was his sex slave and ordered her to call him "King." Kristen cooperated in hopes of satisfying him and going home. She knew it might be her only chance to get out of this alive.

Paul's video camera recorded the sexual encounters. Paul's constant directing of both women as they engaged in various sexual acts could be heard on the audio.

The pretty dark haired Kristen French endured the painful sex inflicted on her. She performed any sexual act the sick and perverse Paul and Karla asked. She allowed them both to abuse her mentally, sexually and physically as they satisfied their own carnal desires. Kristen put up with being berated and degraded. She did whatever they said so they would release her. But after days of beatings, being raped and abused, Paul wrapped an electrical cord around her neck and strangled the pretty 15-year-old girl.

The cold hearted killers, Karla and Paul, after taking the life of a schoolgirl, showered and went to her parent's house for Easter dinner.

When they returned, they washed Kristen's corpse to remove fingerprints and bodily fluids that might be traced back to them. Karla cut off her long brown hair in case it had picked up carpet fibers, and they burned Kristen's clothes and jewelry.

That night they took Kristen's body to an area not far from where they had disposed of Leslie Mahaffy, near Burlington, Ontario. Paul wanted the police to believe they were dealing with a murderer from Burlington to draw attention away from St. Catherine's.

The murdering duo dumped Kristen French on the side of the road where she would not be discovered until April 30, 1992, two weeks after she had disappeared.

The police had two dead young girls. They investigated all clues and tips. Finally a witness came forward stating she saw some people fighting in a car in the church parking lot about the time of the abduction of Kristen French. The woman identified the car as a white Chevrolet Camaro.

One person suggested that a man she knew, Paul Bernardo, would be a person the police should check. Two police officers paid a visit to the Bernardo home while Karla was at work. The detectives questioned Paul and found him to be a well groomed, intelligent, forthcoming, young man and the officers saw the wedding photograph hanging in his living room showing he was married to a beautiful woman. He even laughingly told the police officers that he had been questioned in the Scarborough Rapist case because he resembled the composite drawing.

Paul Bernado did not fit the profile of the man who was murdering young women in St. Catherine, and he did not drive a white Camaro.

When she returned from work, Paul was elated as he bragged to Karla that he had fooled the police. They didn't suspect anything. He told her how he glibly talked to the police and joked about being questioned in the Scarborough Rapist case. Paul told Karla he was too smart to be caught. His ego exploded, he felt he could do anything now and not be caught.

The relationship between Karla and Paul began to falter. He would blow up at her for no reason. He would scream and belittle her and he would beat her. He convinced her that she was the cause of their marital strife. She wanted to keep their marriage together and endured the mental and physical abuse.

Once she tried to leave and he reminded her that he had a videotape of her drugging and raping her sister, Tammy, and that he would show it to her parents. His threat worked and she stayed with him, but their marriage was not based on the love it once was. He told her she was no longer his wife, she was just a sex slave and good alibi if the police would become suspicious of him.

In January of 1993, Paul brutally beat Karla with a flashlight. Both of her eyes were blackened, one eye so swollen it was closed. There were black and blue bruises all over her body and she was in intense pain from the beating. When Paul was out for the evening smuggling cigarettes, Karla searched the house for the incriminating videotapes.

She looked in the rafters of the garage where Paul had once hidden them and she looked in other of Paul's hiding places but could not find the incriminating tapes.

Karla, fed up with being beaten and lying to her co-workers about why she was always bruised, decided to leave Paul, although she had to move fast before Paul returned.

She called her parents, telling them of her decision and asked them to come and get her.

Her parents arranged for Karla to hide out in the home of a family friend until a police officer could meet her. The police officer immediately took Karla to the hospital where she stayed for three days undergoing tests to see if she had incurred any internal or permanent injuries.

Karla filed assault charges against her husband. Paul Bernardo was arrested for spousal abuse.

While he was being held in jail, the Center of Forensic Sciences discovered the blood samples taken from Paul Bernardo almost two years earlier were an exact match to the semen samples collected from three of the Scarborough Rapist victims.

In the course of the investigation, over two hundred blood samples had been collected and sent to the lab for DNA testing. The lab was understaffed and overworked and since the rapes in Scarborough had stopped, the forensics lab only worked on the case when time permitted.

With the assistance of an attorney, Karla negotiated a plea arrangement with the prosecutor. In exchange for testifying against Paul in the murder and rape of Leslie Mahaffy and Kristen French, Karla would plead guilty to two counts of manslaughter and receive a 12-year sentence.

Karla spent days meeting with the Toronto Police, telling them what she knew of the rapes Paul committed in the Scarborough area. She was also interviewed at length by the Green Ribbon Task Force which had been assembled specifically to investigate the murders of Leslie and Kristen.

Karla told the police that there were videotapes that vividly and morbidly depicted the rape and murder of both of the young girls and the rape of other young women that Paul had brought home. The police spent days searching the home but could not find the tapes.

Paul Bernardo told his attorney where he could find the tapes, hidden in a recess in a second floor ceiling, accessible through the light fixture.

The attorney found the tapes and kept them in his possession for over a year, holding up the beginning of the trial. For holding the tapes and not turning them over to the police, the attorney would later be charged with obstruction of justice and possession of child pornography. But he was later acquitted of the charges.

When the attorney resigned from the case, the new attorney turned the tapes over to the prosecutor's office. The trial of Paul Bernardo on nine charges including two counts of first-degree murder in the killing of Leslie Mahaffy and Kristen French began.

During the four-month trial, Karla told the jury about Paul's obsession with young girls and how he would abduct them and force her to participate in their sexual abuse. She portrayed herself as a hapless pawn in her husband's perverted life. She told the court that she couldn't help any of the girls because Paul would beat and possibly kill her as well.

Yet during the trial, the videotapes showed a different view of Karla's involvement. It displayed Karla participating and enjoying the sexual abuse of the young girls. The videotapes showed that the prosecutors might have hurried too quickly to grant a plea arrangement to Karla in return for her testimony. The tapes showed she was guilty of crimes much more heinous than manslaughter. She should have been charged with murder.

Paul Bernardo, on September 1, 1995, was found guilty of all nine charges. He was sentenced to life in prison without the possibility of parole for the first twenty-five years.

After serving her 12-year sentence in various Canadian prisons and mental institutions, Karla Homolka, was released from custody.

The saga of Paul Bernardo continued long after he was sentenced to life in prison. In 2006, Bernardo admitted to being responsible for ten additional sexual assaults. He is also suspected in the 1990 death of high school student Elizabeth Bain.

Karla has remarried and moved away. Paul Bernardo, the psychopathic killer, lives in solitary confinement in jail.

# The Clown Of Death
# - John Wayne Gacy

John Wayne Gacy was an ambitious business school graduate with a strong desire for success. He worked the long hours of retail sales at a men's clothing store and it paid off. Before long he was offered the opportunity to manage his own store in Springfield, Illinois.

Gacy worked the hours required in retailing and to further his career, he became involved with influential volunteer civic organizations such as the Chi Rho Club, the Catholic Inter-Club, Chicago Civil Defense, the Holy Name Society and the Springfield Jaycees. Members of the organizations held John Gacy in such high regard he was elected to assorted administrative offices in the organizations.

The ambitious entrepreneur fell in love with one of his co-workers, Marilynn Myers, and the couple was married in 1964. Marilynn was originally from Waterloo, Iowa, where her father owned several Kentucky Fried Chicken restaurants.

Marilynn's father offered Gacy a job managing one of the fast food restaurants and the young couple moved to Waterloo.

Gacy was an avid student of his father-in-law and learned the food business quickly. Gacy had a desire to succeed and some day take over the chain of restaurants.

Gacy immersed himself in work, but to increase his network of influential business contacts, he became involved with the Waterloo Jaycees.

The United States Junior Chamber (Jaycees) gives young people between the ages of 18 and 40 an opportunity to learn and hone their skills in the world of business through community service.

John Wayne Gacy was on the road he had so anxiously sought. He was married to a devoted wife, lived in a nice house in a good neighborhood, he was becoming a successful businessman and he was a well-respected member of the community through his volunteer work with the Jaycees. The births of his own children, a son followed shortly by a daughter, were two other proud moments of his life. He was on his way to the American dream.

It was a long way from growing up with a drunk and abusive father, a long way from the troubled youth who attended four different schools his senior year of high school.

Despite John Gacy's accomplishments, and never ending enthusiasm for community projects, rumors began to surface about Gacy's sexual preference. Whether working on a Jaycee project or with the young employees who worked at the fast food restaurant, Gacy always seemed to be in the presence of young boys.

The rumors were confirmed and Gacy's ideal life was shattered in May of 1968 when Gacy was arrested for sodomy with a teenaged boy.

The boy, an employee at the restaurant Gacy managed, told authorities that Gacy had tricked him to going to his house where Gacy handcuffed the boy and raped him. Gacy at first denied the accusations then changed his statement, saying the boy consented to the sexual encounter.

While out on bail, Gacy hired another young man to beat up his accuser. The boy was caught and quickly told the police that John Gacy

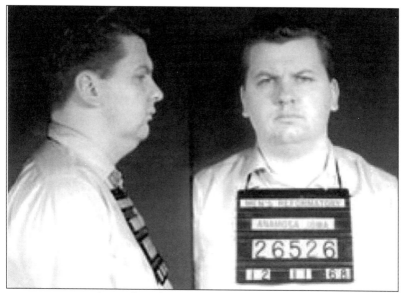

*An early police mug shot of John Gacy.*

had offered to pay off his car payment if he would beat up the other boy.

Twenty-six-year-old Gacy was sentenced to the maximum sentence for the crime of sodomy, ten years in the Iowa Reformatory for Men.

Gacy lost all that he had worked so hard to earn. His wife divorced him, he had no visitation rights with his children, he lost his job at the restaurant and the future possibility of managing if not owning the chain of restaurants and he lost the respect and admiration he sought and had earned in the community. His uncontrolled lust and desire for young boys had ruined his life.

He was a model prisoner and after serving just 18 months of a 10-year term, John Gacy was paroled from prison.

Gacy returned to Chicago where he moved in with his mother and found employment as a chef in a Chicago area restaurant. He was well liked and a good employee. Several months later, John's mother helped him buy a house at 8213 West Summerdale Avenue in Norwood Park Township.

Nobody knew about his past criminal troubles, no one knew he had served time in prison. Gacy's life consisted of going to work and working on his house. That was, until his homosexual desires once again overpowered his sense of decency.

Gacy was arrested for disorderly conduct for approaching a young boy at a bus terminal for illicit sex.

In the busy Chicago judicial system, nobody checked Gacy's past for prior convictions. The Illinois authorities never discovered his arrest, conviction and prison time in Iowa. When Gacy arrived at court for his trial, the witness did not appear. Unfortunately for the boys, since Gacy would murder in the future, the charges against Gacy were dismissed.

In 1972, Gacy married for a second time. His new wife, Carole Hoff, moved into Gacy's Summerdale Avenue home with her two daughters.

John Gacy wasn't content working as a chef. He loved the respect he earned and the challenges of managing a business. After researching various possibilities, Gacy decided to open his own contracting business. He named the company "PDM," for Painting, Decorating and Maintenance.

Gacy poured his business talents into his new career. He secured maintenance contracts and painting jobs. The business prospered and Gacy needed to hire a staff to help so he hired young boys.

Gacy, the workaholic, wasn't an attentive husband, and his mood swings drove he and his second wife apart. In 1975, Carole filed for a divorce from John Gacy.

Despite his marital problems, John was a success in his business life. As he had done in Waterloo, Gacy became active with the community. He became involved with township politics, supporting candidates and working on political issues.

He saw that the candidates commanded the respect and admiration Gacy sought. He decided he would run for public office. Yet he knew before he could be elected, he had to become better known. The salesman in him knew he had to increase his name recognition to get the public to select him over other candidates. He volunteered at the party headquarters and even wore his clown costume to entertain children at party functions. He loved to entertain young children as Pogo the Clown.

Through his work in the local political party, he was appointed to a township commission. He was even photographed at a political function with the First Lady, Rosalyn Carter.

In his own mind, Gacy was on the way to becoming an elected public official. That was until the rumors once again began to surface about his sexual preference. His fondness for young boys again came to the surface.

Gacy often made sexual advances towards the boys in his employ. In one instance, he brought one of the boys to his house. While there, he

*Gacy as Pogo the Clown.*
*From the Author's Collection.*

handcuffed the boy and began disrobing the youngster. The boy worked his hands free and punched Gacy and wrestled him to the floor. Gacy was let up only after he promised he would not make advances towards the boy again.

In a city like Chicago with its large population, it is not unusual for teenagers to leave home. Some run away, some move to other areas of the country for work and some simply disappear. Young boys from the Chicago area began to disappear.

Fifteen-year-old Robert Piest was leaving the drugstore where he worked part time. His mother was in the parking lot waiting for him but he told his mother that he was going to another car to talk with a man who offered him a job working at the man's contracting company.

Robert never returned to his mother's car. Mrs. Piest frantically looked around the store and parking lot, but Robert was gone. The police were called.

Lieutenant Kozenczak of the Des Plaines, Illinois, Police Department was assigned to the case of the missing boy. He discovered the name of the contractor who had offered Robert the job was John Gacy, of PDM Contracting. Kozenczak went to Gacy's Norwood Park home.

The police officer asked Mr. Gacy to go down to the police station for questioning about the disappearance of Robert Piest. Gacy denied knowing the boy but agreed to later meet the Lieutenant at the Des Plaines Police Department.

The police officer searched the nationwide database for any record of a John Wayne Gacy. When he learned of Gacy's Iowa conviction and prison time for sexual sodomy with a minor, Kozenczak requested a search warrant of the Gacy house.

Gacy was not home when the search warrant was executed, but when he found out that several of his belongings had been confiscated, Gacy was furious. He threatened to get an attorney and sue the police department for invasion of his privacy.

The police had strong suspicions that Gacy was involved in Robert Piest's disappearance but they did not have enough evidence to arrest him. One of the items the police found at the Gacy home was a small amount of marijuana, so Gacy was arrested on the charge of possession of an illegal substance.

The police found that three boys on the Chicago missing persons list had worked for Gacy at PDM. The police intensified their investigation of John Wayne Gacy.

With Gacy sitting in jail and no longer a flight risk, the police returned to Gacy's house to search for evidence. They found a ring in Gacy's bedroom that was traced to another missing man, 19-year-old John Szyc.

When confronted with the evidence, Gacy admitted that he had accidentally killed a man in self-defense. Gacy told the police he didn't inform them at the time because he had a prison record and was afraid no one would believe him. He told the detectives that the body of the man was buried below the concrete floor of his garage. But he denied any knowledge of other missing boys.

Before digging in the garage, the police wanted to check out the earthen floor of the home's crawl space. As they lowered themselves into the crawl space they noticed a musky mildew odor that permeated the space. The investigators had to crawl on their hands and knees; having only 28 inches between the floor joists and the dirt floor. Beginning in an area where the soil looked as though it had been recently disturbed, the officer stuck a small folding shovel into the ground and brought up decomposing flesh. The next shovel full brought up a decomposed human arm.

The Cook County Medical Examiner was called to supervise the search. The medical examiner set up a grid pattern to methodically search and document every square inch of the crawl space.

On December 22, 1978, John Wayne Gacy realized that the abundance of evidence was pointing towards the fact that he was responsible for the deaths of several young men. Seeing no way out, Gacy confessed to the murder of the young men.

Gacy described that he would handcuff his victims, disrobe them, and shove socks or the men's underwear down their throats to quiet them while he had sex with them. He told the police he would often strangle the men with a rope or by pressing a board against their throat while he had sex with the men from behind.

Gacy often quickly buried the corpse in the crawl space or sometimes he would keep the dead body underneath his bed so he could revisit it whenever he desired.

John Gacy drew a map of the crawl space showing where the bodies were buried. By December 28, 1978, the Des Plaines Police and the Cook County Medical Examiner reported they had removed 27 bodies from the Gacy house.

During the investigation, two male bodies were found floating in the Des Plaines River. The corpses were readily identified to be the work of Gacy; they both had underwear stuffed down their throats.

Gacy told the police he had disposed of the two bodies in the river because he was running out of room in the crawl space and that he was having back pains from the digging in the confined area.

The prosecutor charged the notorious serial killer John Wayne Gacy with the deaths of the thirty-two men and boys they discovered at the Gacy residence and pulled from the river. Ironically, the body of Robert Piest, the boy whose disappearance lead the police to horror at the Gacy house in the first place, was not found until his bloated body was discovered in the river. He was number 33.

Gacy had confessed to the murder of the men and boys. His defense team could not build a claim Gacy was innocent of the murders with the mountain of evidence stacked against him. Their tactic was to claim their client had killed the men and boys, but he was insane when he committed the murders.

If he were found to be insane while he committed the crimes, Gacy would be sent to a mental hospital until he was determined to be sane. At that time he would be released back into society. If he were found not to be insane while he committed the murders, Gacy would be sent to a prison for the remainder of his life or sentenced to death.

The trial started on February 6, 1980. During the five weeks, over 100 witnesses were sworn in and testified on behalf of Gacy or for the prosecution. Expert witnesses, friends and relatives of Gacy testified that

# Prosecutor tells the jury Gacy is worst of all killers

Gacy was mentally incompetent, while others testified that Gacy was in complete control when he murdered the men.

Gacy was found guilty of murder and sentenced to serve 12 death sentences and 21 natural life sentences. A deluge of appeals were filed in Gacy's behalf not claiming he was innocent but from organizations in opposition to the death penalty. On May 10, 1994, John Wayne Gacy was put to death by lethal injection.

# The Murderous
# Anna Hahn

Statistically, 85% of all serial killers in the United States are men. Anna Hahn, of Cincinnati, Ohio, was one of the few women who earned that distinction and she was also one of Ohio's most notorious murderers.

Anna was born in Bavaria, Germany, on July 7, 1906, the youngest of twelve children. The active and vivacious woman had an affair with a doctor from Vienna, and became pregnant with the doctor's child. The pregnancy brought embarrassment and shame to her parents. They insisted she move to America.

In 1929, 23-year-old Anna, her infant son Oskar, and her husband, the doctor, immigrated to the German neighborhood in Cincinnati, Ohio, where the family moved in with an aunt and uncle. Unfortunately, shortly after they settled in America, Anna's husband died, leaving her a widow with a young child.

Anna met a telegraph operator, Philip Hahn, at a dance and the couple began dating and were soon married. Before long the young couple inherited Anna's aunt and uncle's house.

Anna was never satisfied with what she had, she always wanted more. Her husband's salary was not sufficient to keep her in the manner she liked, so to earn more money she and Philip opened two delicatessens, one for Philip to operate and Anna managed the other.

Anna grew bored with the work involved to make the delicatessen successful. She looked for other ways to get rich quick. It seems she found a successful venture of defrauding insurance companies.

During the period Anna and Philip owned the delicatessens, insurance companies paid out several thousands of dollars for damages from

three fires. One was at the delicatessen Anna operated and two were at their house.

Anna thought insurance was a pretty good idea, such a good idea that she suggested Philip should get a $25,000.00 life insurance policy. He refused. Later she suggested for a second time that Philip needed life insurance but he again refused.

One day Philip became ill. He thought he would improve like he always did but instead he grew progressively worse. Philip's mother, concerned for her son, recommended he go the hospital, but Anna told her it wasn't necessary, he would get better. Philip's mother took her son to the hospital against his wife's protests.

Philip improved but his marriage did not. He separated from Anna before too long.

Anna, separated from her husband, needed to find a way to financially support herself and her young son.

Anna became a visiting nurse for elderly patients. The fact that Anna had neither experience caring for the aged or any training in the area didn't stop her from choosing the career.

An elderly gentleman in Cincinnati's German community, Ernest Koch, was the first to hire Anna Hahn to care for him. Anna didn't work very long with her first patient because before long Mr. Koch became very sick and on May 6, 1932, died an agonizing death.

Despite the short time Anna worked with him she must have impressed Mr. Koch. At his death he willed his house to Anna and her son.

A retired railroad worker, Albert Palmer, next hired Anna Hahn. Anna and Mr. Palmer met at a local horse track and they became friends. As with Ernest Koch, Mr. Palmer became violently ill and died soon after he befriended Anna. Before he died, Albert loaned Anna $1,000.00. It was a loan and she signed an I.O.U. promising that she would repay the money. Yet after Albert Palmer's death, the I.O.U. document disappeared.

In retrospect, one might question the early death of Anna's first husband, the death of Anna's aunt and uncle and the inheritance of their home.

On June 3 of 1937, seventy eight-year-old Jacob Wagner died. He had been ailing when Anna Hahn appeared at his doorstep. She claimed that she was his long lost niece. Although he had told neighbors that he didn't have a niece, he employed Anna to be his nurse. After his death, a will was produced naming Anna as the sole beneficiary to his estate. Anna received $17,000.00 which was quite a handsome sum in 1937.

Olive Luella Koehler was an elderly neighbor of Mr. Wagner. She and the nice nurse who cared for Jacob became friends. On two different occasions Anna took Mrs. Koehler ice cream cones. On the second occasion Mrs. Keohler became ill; so ill that she was rushed to the hospital. It was only later that she found out how close she came to death.

THE EVENING INDEPENDENT, MASSILLON, OHIO

**Anna Hahn Confident She Cannot Be Convicted For Mass Murders**

*Mrs. Anna Hahn, accused of mass murder.*

*George Gsellman, one of Mrs. Hahn's alleged victims.*

*Judge Charles S. Bell, who presides at Mrs. Hahn's trial.*

Anna found the get rich quick scheme she had been looking for. She had received a home from one patient, a $1,000.00 loan she would not have to repay from another and $17,000.00 from her third elderly patient and the fourth man in her care, George Gsellman, died and left her $15,000.00. Anna Hahn had found her niche.

Another of Cincinnati's residents was the next to come under the "care" of

Anna Hahn. George Obendorfer was a sixty seven-year-old Russian immigrant who earned a living as a shoemaker. He had separated from his wife and began seeing Anna.

Anna convinced Mr. Obendorfer that they should take a trip to Colorado Springs, Colorado, to see the ranch that Anna owned. Anna, George and Oskar boarded a train in Cincinnati bound for Colorado Springs.

George Obendorfer, was a healthy, vibrant man, but while on the train he became ill. After arriving in Colorado Springs Anna, George and Oskar checked into the Park Hotel but George's condition continued to worsen, until he was taken to the hospital.

The doctors could not diagnose the illness that had made Mr. Obendorfer so deathly ill. Despite their efforts, George Obendorfer died on August 1, 1937. The hospital notified the police that a man had died under suspicious circumstances.

Anna was not at the hospital when George died; in fact, when she was tracked down, Anna denied ever knowing him. Under questioning by the police, Anna changed her story. She told them that she did know Mr. Obendorfer; they met on the train from Cincinnati.

The police were working another case at the same time; the theft of diamonds from the Park Hotel, the same hotel where Anna Hahn and her son were staying. When the Colorado Springs Police asked at area pawnshops if anyone had tried to sell diamonds, one shop owner told of a woman with a young boy. He later identified Anna Hahn as the woman.

Anna's life began to unravel. The death of George Obendorfer was found to be attributed to poisoning. The Colorado Springs Police contacted the Cincinnati Police with the information and an investigation into Anna Hahn commenced in that city.

The Cincinnati Police discovered that

# HER IRON NERVE AND VANITY GONE AS MRS. HAHN DIES

Woman Was In Mental Anguish, Says Feminine - Writer Who Accompanied Her On Her Last Walk

(EDITOR'S NOTE: Dorothy Todd Foster, Columbus Dispatch reporter, walked to the Ohio penitentiary death chamber with Anna Marie Hahn last night. Altho the newspaperwoman did not witness Ohio's first electrocution of a woman, she has written for the Associated Press her description of Mrs. Hahn's "death hour" reactions).

By DOROTHY TODD FOSTER

Anna Hahn was the care-giver for several area men. Further investigation revealed that some of the men in her care died of unexplainable causes. A judge signed an order to exhume the bodies of some of the men and an autopsy showed the men had died of poisoning.

In Cincinnati, Anna was arrested for the death of her elderly patients. She loudly proclaimed her innocence but after a four-week trial where overwhelming evidence was presented, Anna Hahn was found guilty of murder and sentenced to die in the electric chair.

Anna's lawyers filed several appeals to change her sentence to life in prison, her appeals made it to the State Supreme Court, but ultimately the death by electrocution order was upheld. On December 7, 1938, Anna Hahn was dragged, screaming and crying, by prison guards to the electric chair. She was put to death at 8:13 pm.

After Anna's death, her attorneys sold letters Anna had written to the *Cincinnati Enquirer* with the proceeds being put into a trust for Anna Hahn's 12-year-old son, Oskar. In the letters she confessed to killing the men in her care and men she had befriended.

Anna Marie Hahn had taken the easy way to make a living. She didn't like to work for it; she found it preferable to simply kill others and take their belongings. She admitted responsibility for the premature deaths of five men at her hand. Yet, there are other possible attempted murders and questionable deaths that occurred to those who were unfortunate enough to be close to Anna. Could she have gone to her death with her confession only telling the authorities of some of her horrific deeds?

# The Sparling
# Family Is Dying

"If you seek a pleasant peninsula, look about you."

The State of Michigan's motto aptly describes the two-peninsula state.

The Upper Peninsula is situated between Lake Superior to the north and Lakes Michigan and Huron to the south. The Upper Peninsula is sparsely populated and blessed with vast plush forests of soft and hardwoods, waterfalls and natural beauty.

The Lower Peninsula is bordered by the length of Lake Michigan on its west coast and Lake Huron and Lake St. Clair to the state's east.

When most non-Michiganders think of Michigan, their thoughts are of Detroit, the old industrial town, home of automobile production and unfortunately, at one time, the murder capital of the United States. But there is so much more to Michigan. Most of the state's land mass consists of forest and agricultural land.

Saginaw Bay, projecting from Lake Huron into the state's interior gives the state's Lower Peninsula its distinctive "Mitten" shape.

The "Thumb" area of the mitten, another peninsula, is blessed with rich soil making it some of the best agricultural land in the state. Laying between Saginaw Bay and Lake Huron, the "Thumb's" climate is ideal for crops such as corn, soybeans and sugar beets. Recently, wind turbines have been constructed to harvest the energy of the wind.

In 1908, in the "Thumb" village of Ubly, a small rural farming town, a 48-year-old farmer, John Sparling, took ill after working in the fields on the family farm.

He was bent over in severe abdominal pain. His son's were able to get him home and called Dr. Robert MacGregor.

Dr. MacGregor was the Sparling family doctor but he and his wife, Ida, were good friends of John and Carrie Sparling. The couples socialized and spent time together.

John Sparling's pain ran throughout his body and nothing the doctor did seemed to lessen it or slow its progression. Not being able to help John, Dr. MacGregor sent him to the hospital at Port Huron, Michigan. Within days the once strong, healthy and vibrant John Sparling had died.

The cause of death was determined by the family physician to be creeping paralysis due to acute inflammation of the spine.

After John's sudden illness and death, Mrs. Sparling and her four adult sons continued to work the farm and Dr. MacGregor frequently stopped by the Sparling farm to assist with financial advice and check on the health of the Widow Sparling. The farm continued to thrive and be one of the more profitable in the area.

One piece of financial advice Dr. MacGregor offered was that Carrie Sparling should purchase life insurance policies on her sons. Since the boys were so vital to the operation of the farm, the doctor thought they should be covered under a life insurance policy of $1,000 each just in case something should happen to them. She agreed and purchased life insurance on her sons.

Two years after John Sparling was struck with a sudden strange and fatal illness, the oldest son of Carrie Sparling, Peter, came down with a painful stomach ailment with similar symptoms as his father.

*Dr. Robert MacGregor. From the* Huron Daily Tribune, *Bad Axe, Michigan.*

Peter was working in the fields when he got pains in his stomach and became nauseous. The pains worsened and he was doubled over in pain and dropped to the ground. His brothers quickly took him home and put him in bed.

Mrs. Sparling remembered the symptoms of her husband and called the doctor.

Doctor MacGregor visited the Sparling home over the next few days, checking on Peter's condition. When he did not improve, Dr. MacGregor ordered Peter to the hospital. Despite the efforts of the doctor and the hospital staff, Peter died five days after being taken ill.

The official cause of death was sunstroke and blood poisoning.

Twenty-three-year-old Albert was the next member of the family to be taken ill. In May of 1911, Albert became ill with nausea, severe stomach pains, and vomiting, the same symptoms as his older brother and father displayed before their deaths.

Albert died a few days later. The doctor knew Albert had fallen a few days earlier and determined Albert's cause of death to be the result of a stomach injury he had incurred when he fell.

In a matter of three years, three members of the Sparling family had died a painful and agonizing death. People began to talk. Were the men carrying some virus that remained dormant for decades then became active and killed them? Was there something on the Sparling farm that made the men sick? People wondered if the other Sparling boys, twenty-one-year-old Ray and twenty-year-old Scyril, would fall victim to the mysterious illness.

The two remaining son's of the late John and Carrie Sparling wondered too if they would be the next to die. They didn't have to wait long for the answer.

Just weeks after the death of Albert, Carrie Sparling's youngest son, Scyril began to experience stomach discomfort. Doctor MacGregor came to the Sparling house to examine the boy and he prescribed the boy a bismuth mixture to aid in his stomach discomfort. While Scyril wasn't as ill as the other Sparling men had been, he did display some symptoms similar to his father and brothers.

The following day Dr. MacGregor brought another doctor, Dr. Herrington, to consult on Scyril. Dr. Herrington examined the boy but didn't find him to be seriously ill.

The next day, Dr. MacGregor brought yet another doctor, Dr. Conboy, to the Sparling home for a consultation. The doctors found that Scyril was not improving; in fact, he seemed sicker than he was the day before. He had severe stomach pains, like his father and brothers.

After the examination of Scyril, the doctors conferred in another room. Dr. MacGregor asked Dr. Conboy if he thought the Sparling boy could be suffering from arsenic poisoning? MacGregor also confided to Dr. Conboy that he suspected the other Sparling men might have been poisoned as well. Although he did not say it directly, Dr. Conboy thought that Dr. MacGregor suspected that Mrs. Sparling was poisoning her family, killing her husband and sons.

Dr. Conboy thought the conversation to be quite unusual. He went to the county prosecuting attorney, Xenophon Boomhower. Since three Sparling men had mysteriously died, he was taken aback when Dr. MacGregor had approached him with his suspicions of arsenic poisoning and Carrie Sparling.

The prosecutor, of course, was aware of the Sparling deaths. He had also been made aware of suspicions surrounding the deaths by the late John Sparling's uncle and namesake, John Sparling.

The older Sparling was concerned for the safety of the remaining two sons of his nephew and Carrie. He feared they might meet with the same excruciating death as their father and brothers.

Mr. Boomhower ordered that a nurse be hired to stay with Scyril to make sure he was not given anything that might harm him.

Dr. MacGregor made the arrangements and Nurse Gibbs was brought in from Port Huron.

The prosecutor shared the belief that Mrs. Sparling might be responsible for the deaths. He asked Dr. Conboy to go to the Sparling home to try to frighten Mrs. Sparling into admitting her guilt in the poisoning.

When Dr. Conboy arrived at the Sparling house, he found Dr. MacGregor was already there. Dr. MacGregor seemed surprised, almost agitated, that Conboy was there.

*Scyril Sparling. From the* Huron Daily Tribune, *Bad Axe, Michigan.*

Dr. Conboy told MacGregor his reason for the visit was to throw a scare into the widow. MacGregor told him not to waste his time that he himself had done it just that morning. Dr. MacGregor thought that she was so fragile that she would need to be committed to an asylum within months.

Scyril's condition continued to deteriorate.

Prosecutor Boomhower ordered that if the young Sparling man should die from his infirmity, a full postmortem would be made. He wanted to once and for all get to the bottom of the cause of the Sparling deaths.

A few days later Scyril became the fourth of the Sparling men to die a mysterious death. He succumbed to the agonizing illness that wracked his body with excruciating pain.

Mr. Boomhower was notified by Dr. MacGregor of the boys passing. Boomhower said the county coroner would be at the farmhouse in the morning to perform the autopsy.

That evening, Dr. MacGregor asked Dr. Holdship to assist him in performing an autopsy on Scyril's body. The doctors did not find anything unusual, nothing that would definitely indicate a cause of death.

When the county corner, Dr. Morden, and Dr. Conboy arrived at the Sparling farm, they were surprised to find the postmortem had already been completed.

Mr. Boomhower was angry that his orders were not followed and the county corner did not perform the autopsy. He ordered the coroner and Dr. Conboy to carry out a second autopsy.

In the second autopsy, the doctors found what they considered were discrepancies. They removed several organs from Scyril's body and sent them to the forensic medicine laboratory of the University of Michigan in Ann Arbor, Michigan.

The results from the University of Michigan arrived a few days later and changed the Huron County Prosecutors Office from suspecting a crime might have occurred, to investigating the murder of Scyril Sparling.

The organs sent to the University of Michigan did not display signs of any disease but they did contain traces of arsenic, enough to easily kill a man. Boomhower had the evidence he needed to support his suspicions and ordered the body of Albert Sparling to be exhumed.

After an examination of Albert's organs, the laboratory at the University of Michigan determined Albert's cause of death to be the result of ingesting arsenic in fatal amounts.

John Sparling, the boy's father who had died over two years earlier and the second to die, Peter Sparling, were exhumed. Their remains were examined chemically and microscopically with the results showing no signs of disease that would result in death. The examination did reveal that both men had enough strychnine in their system to kill them. John, Peter, Albert and Scyril were all murdered by poison.

All evidence pointed towards the Widow Sparling. She had access to all of the dead men so she could have easily poisoned them. She had taken out an insurance policy on all of the dead men. She is the only one who would gain monetarily by their deaths. And Doctor MacGregor told others that he suspected her of poisoning the family.

Sheriff McAuley of Huron County began to investigate the deaths of the men. He followed Prosecutor Boomhower's suspicions and began to question the Widow Sparling.

In the course of his interrogation, Sheriff McAuley discovered that Carrie Sparling purchased $1,000 life insurance polices on each of her sons and she was the sole beneficiary of the policies. Further questioning revealed that the life insurance policies were purchased at the recommendation of Dr. MacGregor and purchased from the doctor's father's insurance company.

When asked what she had done with the money she was paid by the life insurance company she told Sheriff McAuley that she paid off farm debts, bought Dr. MacGregor an automobile and purchased the land and house Dr. and Mrs. MacGregor lived in.

It seemed to Sheriff McAuley that possibly Dr. MacGregor had a lot to gain from the insurance payments as well as Mrs. Sparling.

Doctors Herrington, Morden, and Conboy, who had all dealt with the Sparling men while they were ill or after their deaths were questioned by the sheriff. They all reported that at times Dr. MacGregor acted strange and made unusual statements to them about the Sparling men and their sickness and deaths. During an examination of Scyril Sparling, Dr. MacGregor, out of the blue, asked Dr. Conboy if he thought the boy had been poisoned. At another time the doctor hinted that he suspected all of the men had died as a result of poison, and the doctor told a reporter that he wasn't surprised that arsenic was found in the bodies of the men because they were all, the whole family, being treated for syphilis and the syphilis medication contained arsenic.

These statements led the sheriff to wonder if the good doctor might have more than a professional medical relationship with the Sparling family.

In a move that shocked the community, Sheriff McAuley arrested Dr. MacGregor for the murder of Scyril Sparling.

Due to the pre-trial publicity the case generated, the judge anticipated a huge crowd, but because of the dilapidated condition of the courthouse, Judge Beach ruled that the trial was moved to the second floor of the Tribune newspaper building.

As Judge Beach had suspected, the sensational trial would attract crowds like no other criminal trial in the history of the county. People lined the wooden staircase of the building with men and women straining to hear the proceedings. Others stood below on the walk and street listening to comments being relayed from those on the stairway.

During the nearly nine-week trial, it was brought out that the doctor had a financial relationship in the deaths of the Sparling men. He profited from the insurance policies on the men.

*A view of the rear of the Tribune Building where the MacGregor Trial was held. From the Bad Axe Historical Society.*

He was bought an automobile and Mrs. Sparling purchased the home in which he and his wife lived.

Dr. and Mrs. MacGregor took their new automobile on a trip to the east. Mrs. Sparling gave money to the doctor for the trip and more money when they returned.

The hired hand of Dr. MacGregor testified that the doctor had destroyed several bottles of medicine after Albert Sparling died.

The doctor began to make statements that implicated Mrs. Sparling in the deaths. He said he thought she was responsible for poisoning her family. Mrs. Carrie Sparling was arrested soon after Dr. MacGregor for her part in the murders of her husband and sons.

The doctor told Sheriff McAuley that the four sons of John and Carrie Sparling had contracted syphilis and he was sure that the only remaining son, Ray, would surly die from it as well. The doctor told the sheriff that John Sparling also died from the disease and that he had treated Mrs. Sparling for blindness on two occasions brought on from syphilis.

Annie Pieruski, a woman hired by Mrs. Sparling to help with meals and cleaning, testified that Dr. MacGregor made frequent visits to the farm. He often was there under the excuse of needing to treat Mrs. Sparling for an illness of the eye.

Annie told the court that when the doctor came, Mrs. Sparling would go into her bedroom. The doctor would join her in the bedroom and they would remain there behind the closed door for long periods of time.

While neither the doctor nor Mrs. Sparling admitted to having anything other than a strictly platonic, doctor patient relationship, the

evidence begged to differ. The statement by Annie caused a commotion in the already sensational trial.

That a handsome doctor and the beautiful widow allegedly engaged in a torrid love affair resulting in the murder of her husband and three of her sons, was a story that newsmen drooled over. Newspapers from around the country picked up the intriguing story and followed the trial with daily or weekly updates.

The doctors that examined young Scyril Sparling; Dr. Holdship, Dr. Conboy, and Dr. Morden all testified about what they saw and heard. How they suspected the youngest Sparling had been poisoned but could not prove anything. They also told of strange comments that Dr. MacGregor made, comments that implicated himself and/or Mrs. Sparling.

After lengthy and eloquent closing statements by the prosecutor and defense attorneys, the jury retired to determine the future of Dr. Robert MacGregor.

On Friday, June 7th, 1912, Judge Beach notified the attorneys that the jury had reached a verdict.

At 12:15, the foreman of the jury, Robert Bowman, rose and slowly read the verdict.

"We find Dr. Robert A. MacGregor guilty as charged of murder in the first degree of murdering Scyril Sparling by arsenical poisoning."

A week later, Dr. MacGregor was taken to the Tribune building to stand before Judge Beach for sentencing.

When asked if there was any reason sentencing should not be passed, Dr. MacGregor quietly responded: "Your honor, I am innocent. My case is in the hands of my attorneys. I leave it all to them."

The judge said he didn't want to lecture the defendant, he only would issue the sentence in accordance with law and the verdict delivered by the jury.

I sentence you, Robert MacGregor, to Jackson Prison for the remainder of you life for the murder of Scyril Sparling.

The preceding took less than five minutes.

After the sensational trial that was covered across the country leading to the conviction of Dr. MacGregor, the furor seemed to quell. When Prosecutor Boomhower dismissed the charges against Mrs. Sparling for lack of evidence, it created a stir in the county but was hardly mentioned in the nationwide newspapers that earlier had followed the story.

Doctor MacGregor settled into life at Jackson Prison working as an assistant to the prison doctor and in the prison pharmacy.

The attorneys for Dr. MacGregor filed a petition for a new trial in 1912. They claimed a new witness came forward stating he had observed Scyril Sparling consuming large quantities of a patented tonic, advertised through newspapers and sold by traveling salesmen and in general stores. Judge Beach studied the new information and deliberated for weeks before deciding that the new information did not warrant a new trial.

Next, the attorneys for the doctor took the appeal of the conviction and the life sentence to the Michigan Supreme Court. After consideration, the esteemed jurists of the highest court in the state upheld the decision of the lower court. Dr. Robert MacGregor's appeals had expired. As a last ditch effort, the doctor's attorneys wrote to Governor Ferris and appealed to the governor to pardon Dr. MacGregor.

In 1916, Governor Woodbridge N. Ferris decided to investigate the case of Dr. MacGregor.

Several witnesses were called before the governor's investigators. Residents of Ubly and the county seat of Bad Axe traveled to Lansing and some were interviewed in the county.

Governor Ferris called the Warden at Jackson Prison requesting that Dr. Robert MacGregor report to the capital in Lansing without delay and without prison guards. The Governor was convinced that Dr. MacGregor was innocent and after serving four years of a life sentence, the Governor granted him a full unconditional pardon.

When questioned as to what evidence the Governor discovered that had been missed by the jury of the original trial, the appeal and the Michigan Supreme Court, the Governor declined to say.

Dr. MacGregor was appointed the Jackson Prison doctor and continued in this capacity until 1928 when he died of typhoid fever.

The case of the Sparling men dying in rural Michigan created a sensation in Michigan and across the nation as well. Reporters from Detroit were sent to follow the trial and their stories were relayed to newspapers in every major city. The crime contained all of the ingredients that the early 1900 populace yearned for in a true crime story: mystery, intrigue, murder, a good-looking doctor, a good-looking widow, and sex.

If the doctor wasn't guilty of the crimes, who was? It is a question lost in history.

# From Prophet
# To Prisoner -
# Jeffery Lundgren

There are infamous religious cults that make headlines with their actions. The Reverend Jim Jones started a religious organization with a sound basis in conventional religious beliefs, yet the group moved to Jonestown, Guyana, and Reverend Jones kept its followers under control through fear and intimidation. In 1978, when the group was told by their charismatic leader that the world was coming to an end, more than 900 followers drank drug laced Kool Aid to induce death.

In 1997, another cult that made the national and world news was Heaven's Gate. Thirty-nine members of Heaven's Gate, lead by Marshall Applewhite, committed suicide because their leader convinced them that an extraterrestrial space ship, flying protected in the tail of the Hale-Bopp comet, was coming to take their souls to eternity. But first they had to shed their earthly body. They took a mixture of drugs, lay down on their beds and died.

Not all religious groups are cults, but there are some where the ego and arrogance of the leaders gets in the way of the Lord's message.

One religious leader and self proclaimed prophet, who interpreted the Bible to support his own beliefs and lead his followers down the path to murder, was Jeffery Lundgren.

Jeff was born in Independence, Missouri, in August of 1950. His family were devout members of the Reorganized Church of the Latter Day Saints, RLDS, which is a sub-set of the Mormon Church. Jeff and his siblings grew up learning to hunt with their father and studying scripture in the church.

After high school graduation, Jeff entered Central Missouri State University to study electronics. Lundgren didn't excel in his studies, but did enough to stay in school.

While attending the university, Jeff was a regular at the RLDS student house. He enjoyed the fellowship of the other students with the same beliefs and enjoyed discussing scripture. It was at the student house where Jeff met and fell in love with Alice Keehler.

The couple shared the same friends and the same religion and quickly became inseparable. The couple was soon married and Alice was pregnant with their first child.

Being married and trying to provide for his pregnant wife took a toll on the academics of the couple and they both dropped out of college.

In 1970, Jeff enlisted in the United States Navy. The Navy was a way Jeff felt he could provide for his family and learn a trade as an electronics technician. By the time his four year enlistment was up, the couple had another child.

Jeff, Alice and the two children tried to make a life in San Diego but the job prospects and cost of living forced them to move back to Independence, Missouri.

By 1980, the couple had four children and were struggling to make ends meet. Jeff had trouble holding a job; many said it was not his knowledge of electronics and his ability to analyze and repair problems but his irresponsible behavior and lazy attitude that caused him to be let go from many jobs.

He was very active in the Independence RLDS church. The church elders saw that he had a keen understanding of the scripture and asked him to join the lay priesthood.

Jeff Lundgren led Bible study classes that attracted quite a following. He became well known for his knowledge and interpretation of the scriptures and his charisma brought them back.

As his popularity grew, he began to interpret the scriptures differently than what the church did. He formed a splinter group of the Mormon Church and held classes in his home that attracted large groups to hear his message.

Many who attended the scripture lessons believed that Jeff Lundgren had discovered the "Truth of the Scriptures." They believed he was a man of this earth but with a spiritual understanding of a higher magnitude of the scriptures. Jeff believed it of himself, too. Although Jeff didn't say it outright, it was said by his followers that Jeffery Lundgren was, in fact, a prophet.

Among his followers were many of Jeff and Alice's friends from the college days. They attended the classes and fell under the spell that Jeff held over his followers. His followers provided for him, they gave money to support him and his family. Jeff told his followers that they should give him half of their income; in fact, it was their duty to share their wealth with their teacher.

Some of his followers agreed and increased their giving but others felt it was not their obligation and quit attending scripture lessons at Jeff's home. His financial support was dwindling.

To everyone's surprise, Jeff announced that the scriptures had told him to move from Independence, Missouri, to Kirkland, Ohio.

The city of Kirkland, Ohio, is a town with deep meaning for people of the Mormon Church. Joseph Smith, founder the Church of the Latter Day Saints, had a series of revelations in 1832. His visions told him and the church to leave New York State and move to Kirkland, Ohio. There the church should build a temple to serve as the church's headquarters. The temple was completed in 1836.

While living in Independence, Jeff's revelation told his group to move to Kirkland; it was where Jeff, and whoever followed him, would see God.

Most, but not all of Jeffery Lundgren's followers journeyed to Ohio and settled in rented homes that Jeff selected for them.

Jeff and Alice lived in a rented 15-acre farm with a barn and various outbuildings. Some members lived in the farmhouse with Jeff and their four children and all members worked and gave their money to Jeff. Between those who followed Jeff from Independence and those in Kirkland who heard of the prophet, listened to his teaching and were enticed to join him, their numbers swelled to about two dozen.

Lundgren's teaching became inconsistent with the doctrine of the RLDS church. He did not advocate polygamy (although he later took a second wife), but approved sex between himself and his followers. He selected mates for his single followers and performed their marriages. He told some members not to marry a person they were involved with but rather picked someone else for them. One member said the only thing talked about was scripture and sex. The "Prophet" Jeff would use the scripture to excuse and justify anything he wanted.

Jeff was preoccupied with sex. He taught his followers that God approved any kind of sexual behavior. He taught that the women of the group must be carnal, sensual and devilish. They were there to please the men. They even watched movies as a group and discussed how the actresses moved and acted in a sensual and sexual manner so the women could imitate the behavior.

Jeff told the members that he could read minds and see all in the past and in the future. He felt he was indeed a prophet of God, a chosen one, and anyone who followed him would be there to assist God in the second coming of Christ. Anyone else was their enemy.

The church fathers became aware of his teaching and bizarre behavior. They voted to revoke Lundgren's ministerial credentials and to excommunicate him from the church for unchristian conduct. Jeff withdrew his membership in the church before he was excommunicated.

Lundgren's teachings and demeanor changed. He found scripture passages that he interpreted that his group were the chosen ones and that he was the prophet that would lead them to meet God. But, before that, they had to cleanse the church of its sinful leaders. A plan came to him in a vision to forcefully overtake the temple and kill ten selected leaders of the church and anyone else who tried to stop them.

The group began purchasing and stockpiling weapons and ammunition. To prepare for their invasion of the temple, Jeff ordered the members to do calisthenics, watch violent movies, and practice weapon training at local target ranges. They even entered the temple during the night to plan and practice their siege on the church.

Often Jeffery would deliver lessons to his members dressed in a military combat camouflage uniform. He became obsessed with attacking and killing the church leaders who deemed him unfit to minister to the members of the church; the people who wanted to excommunicate him from the church.

Members saw no reason to doubt Jeff's teaching and his desire to attack the temple. He had convinced them that the church leaders had gone astray and were no longer following God's will. They were convinced they were doing what was right for the sake of their Lord.

In 1988, two members of his flock left Kirkland and the group. Jeffery was furious. He ordered that they should die. They knew their leaving might result in Jeffery issuing a death sentence for them and they left without telling him or any of the members.

Kevin Currie left and went to Buffalo, New York. He was deeply troubled about the planned attack on the temple and went to the FBI to report it. The FBI determined it was something the local Kirkland Police should deal with and notified them with Kevin Currie's information.

The Kirkland Police took it more serious than the Federal Bureau of Investigation. The chief brought in Jeffery and interrogated him about his relationship with the church and the reported planned attack.

Another member, who became very disenchanted with Jeff and the group, contacted the Police Chief through a friend and told what she knew.

Jeff Lundgren had a vision that changed the plans of the group. He told them during one of his rambling scripture lessons that in order for them to see God, they would not need to attack the temple, rather they had to cleanse themselves.

He told select members that in a revelation from God he learned that the group must prove to the Lord that they were prepared and willing to do his work. He continued that in order to do that, they would have to kill a family of their own group. They must kill Dennis Avery, his wife and three daughters.

The Avery family was selected because they tithed much of their income to Lundgren but would not turn over all of their money to the group. Jeff was also upset with Dennis because he didn't have a tight enough control over his wife. Jeff thought she had too much say in the matters of their family and in the group.

Jeff taught the group that in order for them to see God in the flesh they must be willing to rid their group of sins and the most sinful were the Avery family.

Lundgren told the group that the Avery children must also be killed, for the sins of the father were the sins of the children, and that the children of evil parents were also evil and must be dealt with accordingly.

On April 17, 1989, the entire group met at the farmhouse for dinner and an evening of scripture lessons. Little did the Avery's know that was the night they would be murdered by the members of the group they worshiped with, the people they shared meals with, the man they called a prophet.

Alice gathered all of the children other than the Avery's, packed them in the car and took them from the house.

Preparations were completed. The men dug a large hole in the dirt floor of the lower western part of the barn. The Avery family were to be taken one at a time, starting with Dennis then Cheryl and then each girl oldest to youngest, to the barn. Jeff's plan was that each of the Avery's would be led to the lower east section of the barn where they would be shocked with a stun gun and their hands, feet, eyes and mouths would be covered with duct tape.

From the east part of the barn the family would be carried one at a time and placed in the pit dug in the dirt floor. Jeff would stand over the victim, point his .45 Colt revolver and pull the trigger. Ironically, Jeff bought the pistol with money Dennis Avery had turned over to the group.

Dennis was first called to the barn under the pretense of looking over some camping equipment with the other men. In the east room of the barn, the stun gun was placed against Dennis and triggered. Dennis did not collapse unconscious as expected, rather he yelled out in pain. The plan was compromised and the men had to improvise. They jumped Dennis and securely wrapped his hands and feet. He knew what was happening and he told them that it wasn't necessary. But his mouth was taped and his pleas fell silent.

Dennis was carried into the larger section of the barn. He was lowered into the pit. With his feet taped together Dennis could do nothing.

As planned, a member started a chainsaw to drown out the sound of the gunshot.

Dressed in military fatigues and holding the Colt pistol, Jeff stood on a mound of dirt waiting for his victim. Jeff Lundgren, the self proclaimed prophet, took aim on the man on his knees in the pit and shot Dennis from behind. As the man lay bleeding in the earthen pit Jeff took aim again and fired another round into the body.

One of the men went to the house to tell Cheryl Avery that she was needed in the barn.

In the east room she was jolted with the stun gun. It had the same effect as it had on her husband. The men were prepared to over power her but instead she was told to "Just let it go."

Cheryl knew what was happening, she relented, and allowed herself to be taped.

She was carried into the other room and lowered into the pit. She came to rest in a sitting position with her back against the wall of the hole. "The Prophet" aimed and shot Cheryl in the back of the head. She slumped dead into the dirt already soaked with her husband's blood.

Trina Avery, 15-years-old, was told her mother needed her help in the barn. Using the stun gun had proved to be ineffective so it was tossed aside. The men began to tape Trina's wrists and ankles while they played word games with her.

Once taped, Trina was carried to the pit containing the dead bodies of her mother and father. She was lowered in and eased into a sitting position leaning against the dirt wall.

As the chainsaw noisily ran, Jeff Lundgren stepped forward and, without saying a word, aimed at the back of the girl's head and calmly squeezed the trigger of the semi-automatic weapon. The bullet missed its mark and grazed the girl's head. The second shot by Lundgren penetrated her skull, killing her instantly.

Thirteen-year-old Rebecca Lynn was the next to go to the barn. She was asked if she wanted to go to the barn to see the horses. She excitedly followed, eager to see them.

Damon, one of Jeff and Alice's sons, warned the others that Becky was on her way. The men taped her legs, hands and mouth then carried her to the pit. She was lowered down on to the bloody bottom of the pit. Jeff shot her in the chest and thigh.

Karen Avery was the last of the family to die. The seven-year-old girl was hoisted up on one of the men's shoulders for a piggyback ride out to the barn.

Damon, as he had for each member of the Avery family, called out to the men that they were on their way. The men could all justify that the Avery family needed to die for the group to be more pure to be accepted by God when Christ made his second coming.

They taped up the child, lowered her into the pit with her dead mother, dad and sisters. Jeffery Lundgren, without guilt or mercy, in cold blood, shot seven-year-old Karen in the head. She died instantly.

Jeff, his work for the Lord done, told the men to cover the bodies with lime to quicken decomposition and to fill the hole. To disguise the fact that the earthen floor had been disturbed, the men placed bags of garbage and other refuse all around.

The next step in Jeff Lundgren's master plan called for the entire group to leave Kirkland. The group had been preparing for a wilderness journey. Jeff divided them into groups that left at various times throughout the night so as not to attract attention.

The group reunited at a location near Davis, West Virginia. They established a camp that resembled a military encampment. Foxholes and trenches were dug and men stood guard against anyone who might try to infiltrate the compound. They even mounted the anti-aircraft gun they had purchased to protect against an assault by helicopter.

Jeff's behavior became more bizarre. He issued an edict that women of the group, married or not, must be cleansed. To be eligible to meet God, the women would have to go through a sexual cleansing by Jeff. He reminded them that anyone not obeying his orders might end up like the Avery's.

After five months at the wilderness compound, weather was cooling and money was running out. Jeff instructed everyone to move back to Missouri where they could stay in a barn owned by a friend.

They stayed only one week in the barn when Jeff told everyone that they should all go their separate ways and meet again in the summer for another wilderness camp. The men were to get jobs and save money to be given to support Jeff, Alice, their family and the group.

Keith Johnson, a follower of Lundgren's, who was riddled with guilt over the massacre of the Avery family, went to the police and told them what he knew about the deaths of the Avery's. He provided the authorities a map of the barn indicating the location of the mass burial site.

The report was sent to the Kirkland Police Department. The department had been curious about the Lundgren group for some time but since they mysteriously disappeared from Kirkland one night, they had nothing left to investigate. With this information, the chief instructed one of his officers to check into the Avery family.

*Jeffery Lundgren, the killing prophet. From the Clark County Prosecutor's Office.*

Not being able to find out anything about them or their present location, the officer went to the barn with a copy of Keith Johnson's map to look around. After moving garbage, he discovered an area of the dirt floor that looked as though it had been disturbed.

The officer notified the chief of his discovery and the Kirkland Fire Department was brought in to excavate the dirt floor of the barn. The firefighters had not dug very deep before a horrible odor began to emit from the soil.

The bodies of Dennis, Cheryl, Trina, Becky and Karen had been found.

As the news of the multiple deaths found in Kirkland, Ohio broke, members of the group began showing up at police departments around the county trying to deal their confessions in exchange for leniency.

Jeff was arrested outside of San Diego, California. Jeff, Alice, and three of their children were all taken into custody for the deaths of the five members of the Avery family.

Jeffery Lundgren, the lazy electronics technician who was let go as a tour guide at the Independence, Missouri, temple for stealing between $17 and $21,000 from the church, was found guilty of five counts of murder and five counts of kidnapping. The jury only took two hours to find the false prophet guilty. For his part in planning and executing the entire Avery family, Jeffery Lundgren was sentenced to five death penalties.

Alice Lundgren was found guilty of five counts of murder and five counts of kidnapping. She was sentenced to 150 years to life in prison.

Damon Lundgren was sentenced to 120 years to life for four counts of murder and five counts of kidnapping

Ronald Luff, the man who carried little Karen on his back to the barn, taped all of the Avery family and carried them to the pit, was sentenced to 170 years to life.

Another member of the Prophet Lundgren's cult, Daniel Kraft, was found guilty of five counts of murder and three of kidnapping and received a sentence of 50 years to life.

Gregory Winship was convicted of five counts of murder. He operated the chain saw to cover the sounds of the gunshots. He is serving a prison term of fifteen years to life.

A sentence of fifteen years to life was handed down to Richard Brand for five counts of murder. Richard was one of the men in the barn that overpowered Dennis and taped the family up prior to their deaths.

Three other members of the group were found guilty of conspiracy to commit murder and sentenced to seven to twenty five years behind bars. They are Sharon Bluntschly, Deborah Olivarez, and Kathryn Johnson. These three women were in the farmhouse the night of the murders and did nothing to prevent them.

Two others, Dennis Patrick and Tonya Patrick, were given a sentence of 18 months for obstructing justice. The sentence was suspended and they were placed on one year's probation. The Patricks were not present at the farmhouse during the murders but were fully aware of the plan.

After being found guilty, Jeffery Lundgren appealed the death penalty. He fought his death penalty on the grounds that he was overweight and the lethal injection of the toxic chemicals designed to kill him would act too slowly and result in a slow and agonizing death.

The prophet exhausted all avenues of appeal and, on October 24, 2006, Jeffery Lundgren was put to death by lethal injection.

# The Madman Of Bath, Michigan - Andrew Kehoe

A tradition in American rural schools was the iconic one-room schoolhouse, a school where one teacher taught students of all grades with the older students helping teach the younger students. But in the early 1900s, a shift in educational thought was towards consolidating the one-room schoolhouses into one larger multi grade building.

Experts of the time theorized students would receive a better, more thorough education if they were kept with students of the same age and educational needs.

The small town of Bath, Michigan, located about ten miles north of state capitol of Lansing was going through just such a transition. The school district constructed a large two-story building to house all grades and closed several small rural schools.

In most small communities, the school was a source of pride. Almost everyone in the community had gone to the school, had children, grandchildren, nieces, nephews, or knew children attending. The school was the thread that held the community together.

As with most large and small communities, not everyone supported the larger school concept. In 1927, many in rural Michigan were still struggling after the 1920 stock market crash and the economic depression that followed.

The State of Michigan finances schools through property taxes and some people, especially the farmers who hold large tracks of land, were required to absorb a larger portion of the cost.

One man in the Bath Consolidated School District who was furious over the high cost of education was Andrew Kehoe. Andrew, together with his wife, owned a farm in the school district and despite his ability to repair almost anything, he was having trouble meeting the mortgage payments on his property. He was in jeopardy of losing his land and home.

Andrew Kehoe was born in Tecumseh, Michigan, in 1872. After his high school graduation he attended college in Lansing, Michigan, at the Michigan State College for a while, but he decided to move west to Missouri where he enrolled in an electrical school.

While at the school, he fell from a ladder incurring a severe head injury. He laid in a coma for several weeks before regaining consciousness. After that experience, he moved back to Michigan and married his long time girlfriend, Nellie.

Andrew and Nellie purchased a 185-acre farm near Bath, Michigan from the estate of Nellie's uncle.

Mr. Kehoe decided to run for the elected position of school board of the Bath District. His platform was one of fiscal responsibility and lowering taxes. He convinced enough people of his concerns to be elected in 1926.

Andrew was very vocal about the increased taxes levied to pay for the new school. In his mind, he blamed the school district for his financial distress. It was that damned new school that was putting a burden on him and causing him to lose his farm. He thought the district didn't need it in the first place; the old country schools were fine. It was the new building causing him to not make his payments to Nellie's aunt and the family was breathing down his neck to pay or face foreclosure.

Kehoe especially blamed Emory E. Huyck for the higher taxes. Since Mr. Huyck became the superintendent of the Bath Schools changes were made. Most thought the changes were needed. To Andrew the changes were unnecessary. They didn't need a new fancy building, and the curriculum had served the students for decades and was just fine. It didn't need changing. Andrew also thought Mr. Huyck spent a lot of money replacing equipment that was good enough for the hundreds of kids who had already passed through the school system.

To complicate his depressing financial situation, Nellie was having health problems that required frequent doctor appointments and expensive hospital stays.

Since Andrew could fix anything, when the school district needed a maintenance man they hired Andrew. With his knowledge of electricity and anything mechanical, he was the best candidate.

Unfortunately, in the sick mind of Andrew Kehoe, he decided he would take care of his problems. He could fix anything and he would fix this, too. He would take care of the taxes, Nellie's health issues and her aunt nagging him about the farm payments.

As the maintenance man for the new Bath Consolidated School building, no one questioned why Kehoe was carrying boxes into the building or why he was often stringing wire throughout the building.

*The Bath, Michigan, consolidated school. From the Author's Collection.*

On May 18, 1927, the last day of the school year, they found out how 55-year-old Andrew Kehoe was going to put an end to his problems.

The meticulous Andrew Kehoe started that morning at his farm. He bashed in Nellie's skull, killing her and putting an end to her expensive medical bills. He callously threw her lifeless body in an old cart and left it behind the hen house.

He sawed partway through the trunks of the fruit trees on the property and secured the animals so they could not escape. He gathered the scrap metal lying around the farm and piled it in the back of his pickup truck.

He had already constructed several homemade firebombs and placed them in each building on the farm. The house, barn, chicken coop, and all outbuildings contained a gasoline filled container with an automobile spark plug attached to it. The spark plug was wired into a battery.

Andrew Kehoe did one last thing. He carefully painted a sign and attached it to the fence of his property. The words painted on the pine board were in Kehoe's mind a justification for the horror he was about to commit; "Criminals are made, not born."

At 8:45 on the morning of May 18, 1927, Andrew Kehoe detonated the bombs hidden on his farm. In a deafening blast, the Kehoe house and farm buildings exploded. Debris from the Kehoe farm was shot into the air and rained down as the house and outbuildings exploded in a huge fireball.

The animals trapped in the barn were burned alive, the fruit trees with their trunks sawn through toppled over, and the fires raged through the building. As Kehoe had planned, nothing would be left standing; everything would be destroyed. Nellie's aunt wouldn't get anything but the charred land.

Kehoe's neighbors came running towards the conflagration as he drove away in his pickup truck loaded with scrap metal.

A second explosion, larger and louder than had destroyed the Kehoe farm was heard. The Bath Consolidated School blew up.

Andrew Kehoe, the school maintenance man, had spent months buying Pyrotol, a surplus World War I explosive similar to dynamite. He told the store clerk that he used the volatile chemical compound to blow tree stumps out of the ground. In actuality, he was placing it in vital locations around the school building and wiring the explosives with detonation devices. He had secretly hidden 1,000 pounds of Pyrotol in the rafters, between floor joists, and in the crawl space, all connected by a mile of wiring.

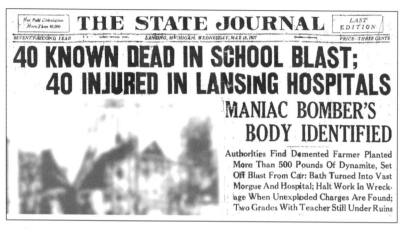

**THE STATE JOURNAL**

*Net Paid Circulation More Than 40,000*

LAST EDITION

SEVENTY-SECOND YEAR · LANSING, MICHIGAN, WEDNESDAY, MAY 18, 1927 · PRICE—THREE CENTS

## 40 KNOWN DEAD IN SCHOOL BLAST; 40 INJURED IN LANSING HOSPITALS

### MANIAC BOMBER'S BODY IDENTIFIED

Authorities Find Demented Farmer Planted More Than 500 Pounds Of Dynamite, Set Off Blast From Car; Bath Turned Into Vast Morgue And Hospital; Halt Work In Wreckage When Unexploded Charges Are Found; Two Grades With Teacher Still Under Ruins

As he drove towards town, Andrew could see behind him his farm fully engulfed in flames. Ahead he could see a thick cloud of dust rising from the school.

At the sound of the explosion, people began running for the school. They were shocked to see the northwest wing of the building completely destroyed. The younger students, grades second through sixth, were housed in that section of the building.

Men and women dug through the rubble of the building to get to the children. Grown men sobbed as they lifted huge pieces of wood and concrete, listening to screams, moans and cries of the injured children buried below. Arms and legs protruded from the debris.

Firefighters and police from surrounding towns and villages and from the State Capital of Lansing arrived on site after hearing the blast. Nobody was prepared for the death and carnage they found. Firemen carried the small, bloodied bodies of dead and injured children from the ruins of the building.

As rescue personnel carefully removed debris to get to the children trapped below, Kehoe parked his pickup truck and watched the commotion. He saw Superintendent Huyck and called him over to his truck. As the superintendent approached, Kehoe lifted a rifle, took aim at the homemade bomb in the truck and fired. The third explosion of the morning erupted. The scrap metal in the Kehoe truck and the pieces of the truck itself were blasted hundreds of feet in all directions, hurling shrapnel in a killing path.

Superintendent Huyck was killed by the flying shrapnel as was Glen Smith, the town postmaster standing nearby. Huyck was killed instantly

*The Bath school after the explosion. From the Author's Collection.*

and Postmaster Smith later died while his wife cradled his bloodied and dismembered body to comfort him. The blast also killed a 75-year-old retired farmer, Nelson McFarren.

Over one block away from the truck bomb when it exploded was Mrs. Perrone of Bath. Shrapnel struck her, ripping her eye from the socket and another projectile lacerated her scalp, penetrated her skull and punctured her brain.

The scrap metal truck bomb also ripped the body of Andrew Kehoe into unrecognizable pieces.

An inspection of the remains of the school found almost 500 pounds of unexploded Pyrotol and hundreds of feet of detonation wiring. The initial blast separated the wiring and resulted in only the Northwest wing of the building being destroyed. Had the explosion happened as Andrew Kehoe had planned, the entire building would have been destroyed, all classrooms, all grades and possibly the lives of hundreds of children.

At the scene, parents joyfully reunited with their children while other mothers and fathers whose children had perished in the travesty, were comforted by friends and strangers.

The injured victims of the blast were removed to hospitals. The children and teachers killed in the blast were laid out in the school playground. Mothers and fathers frantically lifted the blankets covering the faces of the dead bodies looking for their missing children.

One family, Mr. and Mrs. Eugene Hart, discovered three of their five children had been killed in the explosion and the other two were

# Frantic Mothers Search Line At Morgue For Own Children

### Tragic Melodrama Enacted As Women Lift Blankets From Tiny Forms Seeking Their Own Missing Children; Body of Arch Fiend Blown to Bits; Building Torn Apart By Blast Force

hospitalized in critical condition. Four other families lost two children in the tragedy.

In the aftermath of the devastating bombing of the school it was found that 38 children were killed; one second grade student, ten from the third grade, seven fourth graders, six students of the fifth grade and thirteen six grade students.

In addition to the children injured and killed in the bombing, 21-year-old Hazel Weatherby, a third and fourth grade teacher in the Bath school district was found dead in the rubble of the school cradling two of her students. Fifth grade teacher, Blanch Harte, was also killed as she taught her students.

Sixty one others were injured in the explosion and carried the scars, both physically and mentally, for the rest of their lives.

The sick mind of Andrew Kehoe was responsible for the deadliest school killings in the United States. He planned and prepared for months to seek revenge for what he thought was an injustice. He blamed the Bath Consolidated School District and Superintendent Huyck for excessive taxes and the foreclosure on his farm. In his mind, the additional taxes for the new school is what took his farm and he was going to destroy the new school and the children within it.

# The Mad Butcher Of Kingsbury Run

Remember when you were young, walking home from school on a warm fall day? Ambling along in no hurry, maybe kicking a rock, or taking a short cut through a field. Often kids walk along a river or creek looking through the trash strewn about for treasures they could use to build a clubhouse. But most kids never find what two boys found in September of 1935 in the bushes of Kingsbury Run; they found the decaying, headless body of a man.

There is an area of Cleveland, Ohio, called the Kingsbury Run. It is a riverbed, dried up for centuries, that formed a depression in the topography of the city. Since the land was rugged and unusable, it became an eyesore. Refuse was thrown about, houses hastily built by squatters not following building codes, and the people that populated Kingsbury Run were the dregs of society. Homeless men and women, out of work and out of luck, huddled around fires for warmth. The buildings that were in the area were saloons, brothels and a few factory buildings from the previous century now left to decay. The "Run" was not a hospitable place.

The Cleveland Police arrived at Kingsbury Run responding to a call that there was a dead body discovered. The body was of a young white male. His head and penis had been cut off. The police cordoned off the area to look for the body's missing parts.

In their search they discovered another body, also missing it's head and penis. This body showed obvious signs of decay. He had been dead for several weeks.

The men's penises were found lying nearby as if the killer had simply tossed them aside. The heads were found nearby, partially buried.

Once moved to the coroner's office, it was determined that the first body found was of a young man who had died about three days earlier. Fingerprints taken from the body revealed it was the remains of Edward Andrassy, a 28-year-old small time criminal from the Kingsbury Run area.

The second body discovered was that of an older man who had been dead for several weeks. Since he was in a state of advanced decomposition, fingerprints could not be used for identification. The pathologist was puzzled about the discoloration of the torso of the body. It appeared as though the killer had tried to use some chemical to retard the decomposition. It had not worked.

The absence of blood in the soil beneath the men as they laid in the "Run" indicated the men had been killed somewhere else, washed clean and dropped off there. The murderer took the time to pose the corpses. They were both lying on their backs, legs spread with the arms positioned along their sides.

Both men were tied at the wrists and feet and had died as a result of decapitation. The ligature marks on their limbs showed the men had struggled as the murderer methodically sliced through the flesh and muscle of their throats, cut their jugular vein and drained their bodies of life blood. The decapitation showed signs of skill leading the police to

# POLICE BAFFLED AT CLEVELAND IN TORSO SLAYINGS

### Nine Victims of Mysterious Killer Within a Period of Two Years.

**BY DAVID I. RIMMEL.**

Copyright by the NANA (The Lincoln Journal and other newspapers).

CLEVELAND —At the close of two years' investigation into the growing list of Cleveland torso slayings, called the "Kingsbury Run murders" after the section of the city in which the butchered remains of most of the nine victims have been disposed, homicide investigators are still without clues to the motives and identity of the killer who is creating one of the most weird chains of death in modern crime history.

suspect the murderer might be from the medical field, or possibly the killer had gained his knowledge through an occupation such as a butcher.

The police investigated the murders. They talked to known criminals and prostitutes since Andrassy associated with people from that life. While they found several who wished him dead, they didn't find any leads as to who committed the crimes.

Four months later, in January, 1936, a howling dog caught the attention of a woman. She found chained dog barking and trying to get at a basket. With a quick look into the burlap bag in the basket she told a neighbor that it had hams in it. The neighbor looked and corrected her. It was parts of a human body.

The burlap bag contained the body of a woman. Her head, left arm and both legs had been removed.

Fingerprinting of the right hand identified the body as that belonging to Florence Polillo. "Flo," described as overweight and unattractive, an aging prostitute, was well known in the area bars.

A few weeks later Flo's left arm and legs were discovered in the weeds of a vacant lot. Her head was never found.

The Cleveland Police searched for some connection between the murders. At first it looked as though the deaths of the two men, with their penises cut off was the work of a maniac homosexual. But, the murder of Flo didn't follow the pattern. She was female, she was a prostitute, and her genitals had not been mutilated. The case perplexed the authorities.

To compound the investigation all the more, an officer remembered that two years prior a female torso was found floating in Lake Erie. Her legs were cut off at the knees and her head was missing. She was in her twenties and, as with the body of the second corpse found, a substance had been applied to her body in an effort to slow decomposition. The identification of the woman was never made. She was known only as the "Lady in the Lake."

It was in June of 1936 when the killer struck again.

Some young boys found a pair of men's trousers under a bridge in the Kingsbury Run. One can only imagine their shock and surprise when they found the pants were wrapping the decapitated head of a man. The headless torso was found a quarter of a mile away.

From the blood soaked ground around the body, it was obvious the man had been killed at that location. As with the other murders, the cause of death for this man was decapitation.

Torso Victim, Scene of Slaying

*The investigation into the slaying of Flo Polillo. From the* Daily Courier Connellsville, Pennsylvania, July 8, 1939.

The man had several tattoos decorating his body. His identification should have been easily made from the unique body art, but despite the police department's best efforts, the identity of the man was never made. He is still referred to as the "Tattoo Man."

A young girl was walking in the Kingsbury Run when she happened upon the decomposing, headless body of a white male about forty years old. His decapitated head was found nearby along with a bloody pile of clothes. From the amount of blood found on the ground, the man had been killed at that spot an estimated two months earlier.

The next victim was found when a woman tripped over the upper half of a man's torso. The body had been sliced in half. The bottom half of the torso and parts of both legs were found in an open sewer.

The man, in his twenties, had died instantly when his throat was cut through in one stroke. The coroner noted that the dismemberment and decapitation were done with the skill of a person who had knowledge of anatomy.

**The Madman Who Has Committed 8 "Perfect Murders"**

*Mystery of the Killer of Kingsbury Run Who Cuts Off His Victim's Head With One Sweep of His Knife Through the Back of the Neck and Leaves No Clue*

San Antonio Light, *San Antonio, Texas, April 4 1937.*

Cleveland in the mid 1930s was struggling with rampant crime. Gangsters, prostitution, and gambling were openly flourishing in the city. To combat the crime wave, the mayor and city council hired the most prominent lawman in the country. They hired Elliot Ness to be the new Director of Public Safety.

Ness had excelled at cleaning up organized crime in Chicago; he was the man who brought down Al Capone. Now he had the assignment of cleaning up Cleveland. He never expected to become immersed in a case involving a vicious serial killer.

In February of 1937, the next body was discovered. The upper half of a woman's torso was found washed up on the shore of Lake Erie. Her lower half came ashore about three months later. She had been decapitated, but unlike the previous victims, it was not the cause of death. Rather her head had been cut off after she was dead.

A skull was found in June, 1937, and a bag containing the rest of the skeleton was later discovered. Through dental records, it was determined the skeleton was that of Rose Wallace, a black woman who lived in the Kingsbury Run area.

The ninth victim was a man in his mid-to-late thirties. His dismembered body was discovered in the Cuyahoga River. The stomach of the man had been gutted and his heart had been ripped from his body. The man's head nor his identity were ever found.

Victim number ten was also found in the Cuyahoga River. A man saw what he thought was a dead fish. It turned out to be the lower leg of a

The Salt Lake Tribune, *Salt Lake City, Utah, October 18, 1936.*

woman. Several weeks later, two burlap bags containing the woman's torso and parts of her legs were pulled from the same river.

The coroner detected drugs in the woman's system. She might have been drugged prior to her murder or she may have been a drug addict. If her arms had been found, the police might have discovered needle marks, but they never were.

In August, 1938, three men scavenging for scrap metal in the garbage piles of Kingsbury Run made a grizzly discovery, the body of a young woman. Her head, arms and legs surgically removed, were found a few feet away wrapped in butcher's paper and hidden in a wood box. While the Cleveland Police were searching the area for any clues, they found body number 12. Another body was left just a few yards from Number 11.

These two bodies were left in a location that is in view of the office window of Elliot Ness. It was as though the murderer was playing cat and mouse with the Cleveland Director of Public Safety.

The police had interviewed close to 5,000 people during their investigation. Most of the interviews led nowhere. Thousands of police hours were dedicated to the case with little to show. The killer had covered his tracks and managed to elude capture.

There was one man who became of particular interest to the police. The man had the medical knowledge the police suspected the killer had. He had grown up in Kingsbury Run and was well acquainted with the area. The man was Dr. Frank Sweeney.

Dr. Sweeney was born of poor parents and lived in Kingsbury Run as a child. He was knowledgeable of the area, having spent years as a boy exploring and playing in the Run. Frank Sweeney was a medical doctor so he had the medical knowledge and he also had served in an army field hospital during World War I, where one of his main duties was amputating the limbs of soldiers wounded in combat.

Dr. Sweeney was a brilliant man who rose far above his humble beginnings but had recently fallen victim to his own demons. He, as his father before him, was a raging alcoholic. Because of his inability to control his alcoholism, he was asked to leave the hospital, his wife divorced him and the court barred him from seeing his children. This occurred about the time the Kingsbury Run killings began.

Since Dr. Sweeney was the cousin to Martin Sweeney, a congressman who was a very vocal opponent to the seated mayor, Elliot Ness's suspicions of the doctor were kept low keyed. Once he had gathered enough evidence to confirm his suspicion, the lawman invited the doctor to a local hotel to be interviewed. The hotel was selected over the police station so as not to arouse the throng of newsmen camped out on the police station front steps, and so as not to excite Congressman Sweeney.

Elliot Ness interviewed the doctor to no conclusion. The doctor was then given a polygraph test. Polygraph tests in the 1930s were not an accepted practice, but Mr. Ness still had contacts in Chicago and brought one of the polygraph inventors to Cleveland to examine Dr. Sweeney.

Dr. Sweeney sat for two polygraph tests that day and in each instance the test indicated he was indeed the "Mad Butcher of Kingsbury Run".

Shortly after the interrogation and the lie detector tests, Dr. Sweeney checked himself into a hospital. From 1938 until 1965 when he died, Dr. Sweeney remained in various hospitals. The doctor never admitted that he had killed and dismembered the twelve people found in Kingsbury Run, nor was the doctor ever arrested or convicted for the murders. But from the time of his hospitalization in 1938 after he met with Elliot Ness in the hotel, there were no more murders.

There was an arrest in the Kingsbury Run Torso murders in 1939. Frank Dolezal was arrested for the murder of Flo Polillo and he was suspected to be responsible for all of the deaths. Dolezal confessed to the crime but it was generally believed that it was a forced confession and he didn't really have anything to do with any of the murders. Frank Dolezal was found dead in his jail cell before he could be brought to court.

Cleveland had hired the esteemed lawman Elliot Ness to clean up their city as he had done in Chicago, but he met his match with the "Mad Butcher of Kingsbury Run." The citizens of Cleveland were furious that their high priced Director of Public Safety could not uncover the identity of the killer. A few years later when Ness ran for mayor of Cleveland, he was soundly defeated.

The "Mad Butcher of Kingsbury Run" was officially responsible for the disemboweling, decapitation and dismembering of twelve people. Yet some believe that headless bodies discovered in Pennsylvania and dismembered bodies found in New York State and in other Ohio cities were the work of the butcher. The murders were never officially credited to the killer of Kingsbury Run, yet no other murderer was ever charged either.

One of the most infamous murderers in the annals of crime is London's Jack the Ripper. The London police searched for a man who killed and dismembered street women. He disemboweled his victims by surgically removing various organs from their bodies, demonstrating a certain amount of medical knowledge. It is generally accepted that London's Jack the Ripper killed between five and seven women. The "Mad Butcher of Kingsbury Run" killed and dismembered at least twelve, maybe more. The person responsible for the deaths in both cases was never found.

# The Serial Killer Of Rochester, New York - Arthur Shawcross

On the southern shore of Lake Ontario lies the city of Rochester, New York. Rochester is a beautiful modern city with the third largest population in New York State. In 2007, Rochester was ranked sixth out of 379 most livable cities.

Rochester's geographic location on the eastern Great Lakes made it a maritime capital. The Port of Rochester provided access to Lakes Erie, Huron, Michigan and Superior to the west and also east through the St. Lawrence Seaway out into the Atlantic Ocean and the rest of the world.

For a two year period, from 1988 to 1990, Rochester's ideal existence was shocked by a series of atrocious murders. The bodies of brutally murdered women began to be found near the Genesee River. The murderer, Arthur Shawcross, was eventually captured, convicted and sent to prison for the murders.

Arthur Shawcross was born in 1945 in the U. S. Navy Hospital in Kittery, Maine, while his father was in the service. He was a troubled youth. Friends, neighbors and relatives remember him running away from home on several occasions, being teased by other children, breaking into neighbor's homes, stealing from stores, and bullying younger children.

His parents and school authorities were concerned with his odd behavior. Arthur talked in strange voices to his imaginary friends until he was six and wet the bed until he was a teenager. His strange behavior earned him the nickname "Oddie" from his schoolmates. When they teased him, he would fly into a fit. His behavior did not endear him to

his classmates, rather it alienated him all the more. He grew up socially maladjusted.

After his arrest, Shawcross tried to explain his bizarre behavior on events from his childhood. For example, he claimed that as a fourteen-year-old he was having oral sex with his sister, a neighbor boy and others. The participants have denied these claims and their authenticity is in question due to Shawcross' wild imagination and proclivity for lying. But, giving or receiving oral sex, Arthur admitted was his favorite sexual preference. It is believed he preferred oral sex because of his inability to obtain or sustain an erection unless he was inflecting pain on his partner or himself.

As Shawcross was being interrogated for the murders, he told investigators that when he was a young teenager, a man who picked him up, raped him. When he couldn't maintain an erection while the man preformed fellatio on him, he claims the man violently sodomized him.

In 1968, Arthur Shawcross was drafted into the Army. He went through basic training and was sent to war in Vietnam. He claims he took part in several forward operations and during one found two Vietnamese women in the jungle hiding weapons.

He captured the women, killed one, beheaded her and sliced flesh from her thigh to eat. He then raped and killed the other. The reality of the story is in question but by him claiming he had committed such atrocities leads one to question the soundness of mind of Shawcross.

*A police mug shot of Arthur Shawcross.*

He also told of violence he perpetrated against Vietnamese prostitutes while he was on leave. He found them willing to succumb to his perverted desires, easy to victimize.

After his service in the Army, Shawcross held several jobs but was sentenced to five years in prison after he was found guilty of setting a paper mill and the cheese factory where he worked afire. He was paroled early and moved to Watertown, New York where he was divorced from his second wife and married for a third time.

On June 4, 1972 a ten-year-old boy, Jack Blake, went missing. His mother remembered that Jack had met a man, Arthur Shawcross, while he was fishing in the creek near their home. The man had befriended Jack and even went to the boy's house to ask the boy's mother if Jack could accompany him on a day long fishing trip. The mother told Shawcross that she didn't think it a good idea and Arthur left.

Jack's mother went to the Shawcross' apartment looking for Jack the night he disappeared. Arthur told her that he hadn't seen Jack since that morning when he was playing in the apartment complex parking lot.

The boy was nowhere to be found. Police talked to Shawcross but he was just one of many that were questioned. The days turned to weeks, the weeks to months and the boy nor a perpetrator were found.

About three months later, the body of an eight-year-old girl, Karen Hill, was found beneath a bridge. The poor little girl had been raped, mutilated and strangled.

As the police investigated the horrific murder of Karen Hill, they were told that she was seen that morning with Arthur Shawcross. Another witness told police that they had seen Shawcross sitting by the bridge eating ice cream.

While being questioned by the police, with legal council in attendance, Shawcross negotiated a plea bargain with police. He would admit to killing the girl in exchange for being charged with one count of manslaughter. The agreement also included the stipulation that he would not admit or be held responsible for the death of ten-year-old Jack Blake but he would show the police where the body of the boy was buried.

An autopsy and Shawcross' confession revealed that Jack had been sexually assaulted, strangled and his head was bashed in with a blunt object. Furthermore, Jack's heart had been ripped from his body and his genitals viciously cut off. Much later Shawcross told psychiatrists that he had eaten the genitals and heart. He also admitted to visiting Jack's body on several occasions and having sex with the corpse.

In 1972, Arthur Shawcross was sentenced to twenty-five years in prison for the death of Karen Hill.

At first Shawcross had some problems adjusting to prison life. Since he was a child molester and child killer, he was a man with a target on his back. In the hierarchy of prisoners, those who committed crimes against children were the worst of the worst, men who deserved to die a long and painful death.

After a few years, Arthur Shawcross blended into the rest of the prison population and became, to authorities, a model prisoner. In March of 1987, only fifteen years after sadistically raping and maliciously murdering two children, Arthur Shawcross was found to be mentally sound and ready once again to join society.

After his release, Shawcross found housing and employment in various small communities but as soon as his past was discovered, he was driven out of town under threats to his life. He eventually ended in the larger city of Rochester, New York.

On a February, 1988, night, in a borrowed car, Shawcross drove to Lake Avenue where prostitutes were known to frequent. He was hailed by one of the women, twenty-seven-year-old Dotsie Blackburn, and arranged to meet her in a parking lot. She agreed to his sexual request and a price was settled upon.

As they performed mutual oral sex in his car he claims she bit his penis so he bit her vagina. The two fought and he overpowered and strangled her. He dumped her body off a bridge into the icy waters of the Genesee River.

She was found in the river a month later. Despite the time from her death to her discovery, her body did not decay due to the cold water. But because of its long emersion in water the coroner could not find any fingerprints or other evidence on Ms. Blackburn's body.

The coroner was able to determine that she had died from suffocation due to strangulation and that there was a piece of her vagina ripped or bitten off.

Arthur Shawcross was a frequent visitor to Lake Avenue's working women. Most of the time he had sex with them but when Arthur couldn't control himself, he took out his deviant sadomasochistic urges on the women.

His next Lake Avenue victim was Anna Marie Steffen. In the borrowed car, Arthur struck a deal with Anna Marie for sexual favors and drove to a parking area by the river to complete the business arrangement. When he wasn't able to get an erection, she began to tease him and he responded as he had when the school children teased him; he flew into a rage and started punching her. Then he held her head below the river until she was dead.

After a several month hiatus from killing, Shawcross gave in to the urges again in June of 1989. This time he was fishing in the river with a female friend of his, Dorothy Keller. They were in a densely wooded area and after having sex, the two began to argue. Arthur became furious, picked up a log and struck her in the side of the head caving in her skull. He hid her body in underbrush and went on his way.

Patricia Ives, a twenty-five-year-old prostitute from Lake Avenue was the next to die at the hand of the serial killer. According to Shawcross, he and Ms. Ives went to a construction site for sex. While in the act, he caught her trying to steal his wallet. This infuriated him to the extent that he beat her to the ground, sodomized her and strangled her.

Arthur was able to contain his demons for two months but Francis Brown, a twenty-two-year-old prostitute, had a date with him and it ended terribly for her. Arthur choked her, then had oral sex with her corpse.

His sixth victim, 30-year-old June Stotts, was a friend of Arthur's girlfriend. He claims that while he was having sex with June she started screaming so he covered her mouth with his hand and inadvertently smothered her. He hid her body under some brush and cut open her torso so she would decompose faster.

Arthur Shawcross, the newspapers called the "Rochester Night Stalker," the "Rochester Strangler" and the "Genesee River Killer" was not done yet with his deadly ways. His seventh victim was Maria Welch, a twenty-two-year-old prostitute.

Victim number eight and nine were Darlene Trippi, 32, another Lake Avenue woman and after having oral sex with Elizabeth Gibison,

Shawcross snuffed out her life. Kimberly Logan was number ten. Eleven, June Cicero, was killed as the others had been. The final death, number twelve by Arthur's hand, was another Lake Avenue woman named Felicia Stephens.

Shawcross justified each of the deaths by saying the women had angered him by trying to steal his wallet or because they ridiculed him for his inability to get an erection. However, Arthur Shawcross had killed the twelve women and mutilated some of them for his own selfish pleasure.

On January 3, 1990, Arthur parked on a bridge crossing Salmon Creek. From there he could look down on Jean Ciceros's body frozen beneath the ice. He stared down at her and fantasized about killing her and how he returned to her body days later and cut her vagina from her frozen body.

He didn't know that a police helicopter was patrolling the area. The helicopter pilot saw his car parked on the bridge, then noticed Jean's frozen corpse in the ice. At hearing the sound of the police helicopter, Shawcross got in the car and drove off. He was followed from the sky and observed driving into a senior care home where he parked and went inside.

# The Serial Killer Of Rochester, New York

The police squad car, following directions from the helicopter, parked alongside the Shawcross car and went inside to inquire who had just entered. They questioned Arthur about why he was parked on the bridge and where he had been when some of the women disappeared. After several hours of interrogation, he finally told the detectives that he had killed the women. He told them dates, times and details that only the killer would know. The police had caught the "Rochester Night Stalker," the "Rochester Ripper," the "Genesee River Killer".

At his trial, Arthur Shawcross pleaded guilty but insane. The jury agreed he was guilty but despite the expert witnesses his attorney paraded through the courtroom who said Shawcross was insane, the jury determined he was sane. The judge sentenced Arthur Shawcross to 250 years in the Sullivan Correctional Facility.

The citizens of New York State were outraged that a man who savagely beat, raped, murdered and dismembered two small children had been earlier able to negotiate such a minimal prison term and be released from prison back into society to kill again.

The murdering, raping cannibal remained imprisoned until November 10, 2008, when he died of natural causes.

# The Monster of Philadelphia - Gary Heidnik

The sign on the house at 3520 North Marshall, Philadelphia, Pennsylvania, read, "United Church of the Ministers of God." It was the house of the Bishop Gary Heidnik, the minister of the church.

Once it had been a predominately German neighborhood but in the late 1980s it was considered a slum. The homes once built by craftsmen were now run down, the inhabitants, once proud immigrants, were replaced by the down and out of Philadelphia's society.

The church met regularly each Sunday and its congregation was made up primarily of the Black population from the immediate neighborhood. Bishop Heidnik seemed to take a special interest in the mentally challenged residents as it was his calling to be the pastor to the less fortunate.

The Bishop was not always a religious leader; in fact, he had quite a past. He was an intelligent young man yet the victim of a horrible family life. His father was an alcoholic who beat him, his brother and their mother. To free herself of the beatings, Gary's mother killed herself. The boys were left alone with their father.

In the 1960s, Gary joined the Army and was stationed in Germany as a medic. He didn't adjust well to military life and had a nervous breakdown. The Army doctors were so concerned about Gary Heidnik's mental condition they recommended that he be medically discharged and given a full disability. For the rest of his life, he would receive disability benefits from the government.

The Bishop's church was in a rundown part of the city and frequented by outcasts of society but he was a wealthy man. He had turned his

# Great Lakes Serial Killers

disability payments and the meager money from the collection plate of his church into a small fortune. He had a talent for picking stocks. In short order he had amassed a quarter of a million dollars.

The one extravagance he allowed himself was automobiles. He would wear old tattered clothes but he would drive beautiful expensive cars. He had a customized van, a Lincoln Continental, a Rolls Royce, and a brand new Cadillac Coup De Ville.

No one in the neighborhood would have guessed the Bishop was rich, his hair was unwashed and matted and his full beard unkept.

It wasn't until March 24, 1987, that anyone paid much attention to the Bishop Gary Heidnik. That was the night that a hysterical young woman told police about the real Gary Heidnik.

She told the police that she had been held captive by the Bishop for four months, chained to a pipe in his basement. Heidnik used her as his sex slave, defiling her daily, and if she did not do as she was told, he would beat her with belts and rods. The welts on her wrists and ankles testified to the fact that she was telling the truth.

She told the police that she was not the only girl Gary Heidnik was keeping captive. She was the first but there had been others.

The girl, Josefina Rivera, admitted she was a part time prostitute and told the police the horror she and others had lived under the control of the Bishop Gary Heidnik.

Josefina told the authorities that on the night of November 26, 1986, a Cadillac Coup De Ville rolled up next to her and asked if she was working.

*A police mug shot of Gary Heidnik after his arrest.*

She got in the car and they drove to Gary Heidnik's house. In an upstairs bedroom they had sex. Afterwards, as she began to dress, Heidnik grabbed her around her throat and squeezed until she passed out. When she came to, he had handcuffed her and dragged her to the basement. Dressed only in her blouse, the Bishop chained her to a pipe.

The basement was cold and damp and furnished with only a mattress, pool table and washing machine. Near the mattress was a four foot deep hole Heidnik had dug out of a dirt portion of the basement floor. The pit, as he called it, was for discipline.

When she screamed, he beat her and threw her into the pit, covered the pit with a piece of plywood and left her there laying almost nude in the cold freshly dug dirt.

When Josephine awoke, she heard the sound of chains dragging on the concrete floor of the basement. When the plywood was removed from the pit, she saw that Heidnik had another slave.

The new girl was Sandy Lindsay, a 25-year-old mentally challenged woman who Heidnik had befriended several years earlier. Both women were ordered to the mattress and Heidnik had sex with both women. Over the next several days, he repeatedly raped one or the other or both of the women.

Nineteen-year-old Lisa Thomas was the next to fall victim to the vicious rapist. She was raped by Heidnik, handcuffed and led to the basement where she joined the rest of the Heidnik's sex slaves.

Heidnik continued to add to his collection of women kept in his basement dungeon. Deborah Dudley resisted as she was being chained up and paid for it with a beating that left her unconscious.

The fifth of Heidnik's harem was an eighteen-year-old girl, Jacqueline Askins. She, as all of the rest of the sex slaves, was chained to the iron pipe and forced to have sex with the slave master at his whim.

The women begged for food, the meager rations he gave them weren't enough. To accommodate their needs, he opened cans of dog food and

183

*Metro/State*

THE TIMES, FRIDAY, APRIL 24, 1987          3

## Gary Heidnik ordered held on murder-rape charges

RIVERA          HEIDNIK

placed it in front of them. It was another way that Heidnik showed his captives that he controlled them. It was he that decided if they lived or died. Starving, they ate it.

In February of 1987, Sandy Lindsay had angered the "Master." As punishment, Heidnik handcuffed her to the pipe. She hung from her wrists, nude, cold and hungry.

Satisfied that the display had sufficiently warned the other girls that they should not make him mad, Heidnik unchained Sandy and tossed her into the pit. She laid there a beaten woman, demoralized, mentally exhausted and physically broken. She died laying on the cold ground in the pit.

Heidnik was angered by Sandy dying. It wasn't in his plan. He had deemed that she would become pregnant and bear his child. Now she died and wrecked his plans. He dragged her lifeless body from the pit upstairs to the kitchen.

Josefina told the police that the girls later heard the sickening sound of a power saw as Heidnik cut up Sandy's body.

The sociopath skinned some of the flesh from Sandy's legs, chopped it up and put it in a food processor. Heidnik then mixed the chopped human flesh with dog food and served it to his sex slaves in the basement. Other parts of Sandy's body, parts of her legs, arms and hands were stored in the refrigerator for later use.

Josefina convinced Heidnik that he could trust her, that he needed to keep her alive so she could keep watch over the other women and help him find new girls.

He agreed because after all she had been his slave the longest and knew him best. She would be helpful in watching the girls while he was away from the house. She could help him expand his collection of slaves.

Deborah Dudley had been the biggest problem for Heidnik. She talked back, she fought him, and she was not the willing slave he had hoped her to be. To convince her that she must be obedient, Heidnik dragged her from the basement dungeon up to the kitchen. He showed her a large pot simmering on the stove. As she looked inside the pot she nearly fainted. Floating in the pot was the severed head of Sandy Lindsay.

In the insane world of Gary Heidnik, he devised a way to keep the girls under his control. He forced Deborah, Jacqueline, and Lisa into the pit. He covered the pit with the sheet of plywood and ordered Josefina to fill the pit with water from the garden hose.

As the level of water rose in the pit the women were screaming and clawing at the plywood, fearing he was trying to drown them. They pushed against the plywood cover, but the weights Heidnik had placed on it prevented the girls from moving it.

Heidnik took an electrical wire, one end stripped of insulation, the other end plugged into an outlet. He slipped the bare copper wire through holes drilled in the plywood. It was Deborah who was first touched by the wire. She screamed in excruciating pain and fell forward in the water, dead.

Gary Heidnik had ridded himself of his troublemaker and made a statement to the other women that if they questioned him, or in anyway angered him, they would die a painful death. He demanded obedient women.

Deborah's body was put into the freezer. He later buried Deborah Dudley's body.

With two of his sex slaves dead, Heidnik needed to find more women. He took Josefina on a cruise looking for girls to add to his harem.

Gary Heidnik, a white man, preferred black women, as all his slaves were. Gary and Josefina cruised around the streets until they saw a young prostitute, Agnes Adams.

Heidnik negotiated a suitable price for her services and he and Josefina drove her to the North Marshall house. Agnes became the sixth captive of Gary Heidnik.

Gary repeatedly raped and beat the women, making every day for them a living hell. They went hungry, they suffered from their cold and damp confines, and each feared they might be the next victim of the madman, the next head boiled on his stove, his next meal.

On March 24, 1987, Gary again took Josefina out cruising for another victim. By this time, Heidnik was sure he could trust Josefina. She was

# Philadelphia House Of Horrors
# Revelations Grow More Gruesome

his favorite. He had taken her out for dinner, she shared his bed on occasion and she never attempted to escape. He could trust her.

She asked Heidnik if she could visit her family. If he let her, she promised to find a beautiful black girl to join his collection of sexual servants. He trusted Josefina. He believed she would find him a new woman so he dropped her off near her home and they agreed to meet at a nearby gas station at midnight.

As soon as she was clear of Heidnik's sight, she ran to her boyfriend's house and told him her tale of horror. The police were called and she repeated the story for them.

As Gary Heidnik waited at the gas station at the appointed time, Josefina didn't show, rather it was the police who approached his Cadillac with weapons drawn.

Gary Heidnik was taken to the police station for questioning.

By 4:30 am, the police had secured a search warrant for Heidnik's house and several officers where prying the front door open. When they entered, they were overcome with the stench of rotting flesh that permeated the house.

Following Josefina's information, they went to the stairs leading to the basement. There the police found two women huddled together on the mattress. The women screamed and cried hysterically. The officers tried to comfort them and tell them that the horror they had endured was over, that they were safe now.

The two women told the police that another woman was in the pit. The bags of dirt weighing down the plywood were removed and the plywood moved aside to reveal a naked woman crouching on the cold dirt floor of the pit. The woman's feet were chained and her arms were handcuffed behind her back.

The police opened the refrigerator door and found, in plain sight lying on a shelf, a human arm! On another shelf were bags of meat, which turned out to be parts of Sandy's legs and arms.

The pot on the stove contained a putrid smelling viscous liquid. It was later determined to be what remained of the flesh boiled off of Sandy's skull. The food processor still had hunks of human flesh on the blades and a plate in the oven had the remains of cooked ribs; Sandy's ribs.

Even the most hardened of the police officers had trouble absorbing all they saw, but when one of Heidnik's two dogs walked into the kitchen with a human leg bone in is mouth, some ran for the fresh air outside.

Gary Heidnik's trial was short. On June 20, 1988, he was found guilty of eighteen counts of murder, rape, kidnapping, assault, and committing deviant sexual acts. He was sentenced to death by lethal injection. No appeals were granted and on July 6, 1999, Gary Heidnik, the Bishop of the United Church of the Ministers of God, was put to death.

# Killer Without
# A Conscience -
# William Heirens

He was not the child of abuse, he was not raised in poverty, he was not learning disabled, and was not the product of a broken home.

William Heirens was the son of parents who loved and cared for their son. His mother took in sewing to make extra money so William could go to good schools. William was not the stereotypical murderer.

In school, William was liked and had friends but few if any intimate friends. He preferred to be by himself. He also liked to steal things from homes in his neighborhood.

At age thirteen, William was arrested for the first time. A policeman found him in possession of a loaded pistol. The officer took him home and a search revealed the loot William had taken from the homes, stores and apartments he had burglarized.

When he was confronted with the evidence, William confessed that he was guilty of eleven burglaries.

The juvenile was given a psychological examination and it found that William didn't steal for profit, rather he broke into homes and stole things for fun and excitement.

The Judge sent William to a school for juvenile offenders. He went for a year to the Gibault School for Wayward Boys in Terre Haute, Indiana.

William Heirens was not rehabilitated. Just over a year later he was caught breaking into homes again. The fourteen-year-old boy again confessed to the robbery of five homes since he returned from the school for juveniles.

His parents pleaded with the judge to allow them to enroll William in a private school, St. Bede's in Peru, Illinois. The judge was

# Great Lakes Serial Killers

apprehensive because the school was not a correctional school, but relented and agreed.

William excelled during his high school years. The teachers praised him for his intelligence and quick mastery of the curriculum. He was such a brilliant student that when he graduated from the school he was accepted into the University of Chicago as a sophomore, skipping his freshman year all together.

Seventeen-year-old William lived in a dormitory at the university and seemed dedicated to his academic pursuits. But when not attending classes or studying, William participated in the hobby that he had since he was in his early teens. He was burglarizing homes and apartments in Chicago.

On the city's north side lived 43-year-old Josephine Ross who shared an apartment with her two daughters. Josephine's daughters had gone off to their jobs but she remained home. She was out of work and since she didn't have a job to go to, after her daughter left she often went back to bed. She thought that maybe she would take a nap then go take in a movie. But on that fifth day of June, 1945, her day was not going to go as planned.

Around 1:30 that afternoon Josephine's daughter Jacqueline came home for lunch.

As soon as she opened the door of the apartment she knew there was a problem; the apartment was in shambles. Drawers had been pulled from the dressers and their contents dumped on the floor. Chairs were knocked over and newspapers were thrown about.

She walked into her mother's bedroom and into a nightmare. Her mother's lifeless body was sprawled across the bed. She had been brutally stabbed multiple times, her head wrapped in a dress. Blood was splattered on the bedroom walls, window drapes, and other furnishings, and the mattress beneath her was soaked in dark red coagulating blood that had seeped from the gapping gash in her throat.

The police searched the apartment for evidence that would lead them to the person responsible for the gruesome murder. Nothing was missing except a little change and no fingerprints were found.

William Heirens had seen the daughters leave the apartment. Theorizing the apartment was empty, he entered looking for valuables to steal. Instead, he found the sleeping Josephine. She awoke and confronted him and he took the knife from his pocket and stabbed her.

Heirens had found breaking into other peoples house fun and exciting, but now he had discovered that murdering a woman also gave him a thrill. From the multiple stains of ejaculate found throughout the apartment, the murder gave him an intense sexual thrill.

It wasn't until December 10, 1945, when Heirens would kill again when he gained access to room 611 on the sixth floor of the Princess Apartments on Pine Grove Avenue by climbing the fire escape.

As he searched for valuables in the room, he found 33-year-old Frances Brown asleep. He covered her head with a pillow to muffle her screams, drew a pistol from his coat pocket and shot twice hitting Miss Brown in the head and arm.

He easily overpowered the woman who was just over five feet tall and weighed only 95 pounds.

Heirens beat her with his fists about the head and torso, and then in a rage took a butcher's knife to the corpse, stabbing it in the chest and neck. He dragged the bloody dead body of Miss Brown to the bathroom, leaving a trail of red on the floor.

The next morning a cleaning lady noticed the door to room 611 partially open and a radio playing loudly. She peered in the door and saw the room in chaos. She went in and saw the trail of blood. She followed it into the bathroom and found Frances Brown.

Her nude bloody body was draped across the bathtub, her head covered, her pajamas ripped to shreds lay around her ankles. Protruding from the back of her neck was a ten-inch knife. It looked as though William Heirens had laid Frances's body across the bathtub to catch the blood as he hacked at her neck attempting to cut off her head.

Before he left the apartment, Heirens scribbled a note in the victim's lipstick: *"For heavens sake, catch me before I kill more. I cannot help myself."*

The note in large letters, half printed, half in cursive, was scrawled on the wall of the apartment.

A neighbor of Miss Brown reported to the police he thought he heard a gunshot about 4:00 am. The night clerk at the Princess Apartments told police at around 4:00-4:30 am a man came down the elevator, went to the front door and left the building.

The police were now dealing with two murders. Murder was not unusual in a city of millions, but the savagery of the attacks on the women was appalling. The citizens were demanding the police find the sick fiend who continued to beat and stab the corpses of the women long after they were dead. The beast must be stopped, in his own words, before he kills more.

Just after a month of the brutal death of Miss Brown, William Heirens murdered again.

# Search Spreads For Maniac Lipstick Killer

CHICAGO, Dec. 11—(U.P)— Police searched Chicago's north side today for a demoniacal murderer who scrawled a message in lipstick on the wall of his victim's apartment indicating he had killed before and would kill again.

On the morning of January 7, 1946, James Degnan went to his seven-year-old daughter's bedroom. The door was closed, which was something she never did. He pushed open the door and a burst of cold January Chicago air met him. The window was wide open. Suzanne was gone.

A frantic family searched the house and looked outside, but the little blond hair, blue-eyed girl was nowhere to be found.

On the floor of her bedroom was discovered a crumpled piece of paper. Scrawled on the paper was: *"Get $20,000 ready & wait for word. Do not notify FBI or police. Bills in $5's and $10's"* On the back of the paper Heirens wrote, *"Burn this for her safety."*

The police found several fingerprints on the ransom note: the parents of the girl, police officers that handled the note and a few that they could not determine.

Police en masse searched the neighborhood. A ladder, stolen from a nearby florist, was found lying near the girl's bedroom window.

The police went door-to-door searching for any sign of the little girl. In the alleyway of an apartment building a few blocks away from the Degnan house, the police found a pushcart covered with blood, bits of flesh and blond hair.

An anonymous caller told the police to look in the storm sewers near the Degnan house. Officers walked the neighborhood looking at sewers. One heavy cast iron sewer top looked as though it had been moved. They shifted the top to the side and shined their lights down into the dark circular pit.

The men at first could not believe what they had discovered; it was the severed head of the missing child.

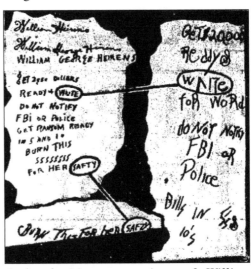

Police officers and Chicago sewer workers worked the night through looking for more of the child. Five hours after the discovery of the child's head, her left leg, cut off at the thigh, was found in an alley. The right leg and parts of her torso were removed from another sewer. The rest of the torso less the arms was found in a sewer less than a block from the house. Little Suzanne's arms were not found for several days.

*A handwriting comparison of William Heirens writing on the left and the ransom note found at the Degnan house on the right.*

The Cook County Coroner, Dr. Thomas Carter, conducted a thorough examination of the remains of Suzanne Degnan and announced that the child had been sexually assaulted and strangled by her murderer before she was callously dismembered with an axe or meat cleaver.

The citizens of Chicago were outraged and demanded that the malicious killer be found before he kidnapped, raped and killed other young girls. The Chicago Police Chief assigned every available officer to work on the Suzanne Degnan case.

The fingerprints found on the ransom note were compared against those of thousands of criminals. It was a slow methodical process done by a trained expert, each print had to be compared against the suspect's print, one by one.

Five months later, the police were called to a possible breaking and entering. Two officers trapped the criminal in an outdoor stairway. The suspect pulled a pistol from his pocket and fired at one of the police officers. The gun jammed; it didn't fire. He pulled the trigger again with the same result.

The officer grabbed Heirens as he tried to escape. A third officer observed the fracas from a railing above. He threw three clay flowerpots at Heirens, striking him in the head. Heirens fell to the ground.

Heirens was arrested for burglary and attempted murder of the police officers. While in the hospital with head injuries from the flowerpots, his fingerprints were taken. As a matter of course the fingerprints were

compared to those from the ransom note. Heirens prints had several points that were identical to the unusual points found on the ransom note. The police were confident they had found the man who had raped, murdered and butchered seven-year-old Suzanne Degnan.

As the evidence against William Heirens mounted, he admitted his guilt and confessed to the murder of Josephine Ross, Frances Brown and Suzanne Degnan.

Heirens confessed to save his own life. In return for his confession, Heirens would receive a life sentence as opposed to the death penalty.

William Heirens requested parole from the Illinois correctional system in 2007. Then he was 78-years-old. At that time he had served 61 years, the longest prison term of any prisoner in Illinois. He received the same decision as he had in the other almost 30 parole petitions... denied.

As of this writing William Heirens remains in the Dixon Correctional Center in Dixon, Illinois. He has long ago recanted his confession and claims he did not commit the atrocities of which he was convicted.

# References

## Only One Survived The Night Of Horror - Richard Speck

*Chicago Tribune*, Chicago, Illinois, July 14, 15, 16, 17, 18,1966

Court TV's Crime Library, "Richard Speck" Connie Fillippelli,
<http://www.crimelibrary.com/serial_killers/predators/speck>

*Crime Magazine: An Encyclopedia of Crime,* "Richard Speck," David Lohr, August 20, 2006.
<http://www.crimemagazine.com>

*Seize the Night,* "Richard Franklin Speck," Kristi and Mark Pisher,
<http://www.carpenoctem.tv/killers/speck.html>

*Southern Illinoisan*, Carbondale, Illinois, July 18, 1966

*Time Magazine*, "Crime: One by One," Friday, July 22, 1966

*The Des Moines Register*, Des Moines, Iowa, July 18, 1966

## The Murder At The Privacky Home - Seth Privacky

CBS News, *A Nightmare in Muskegon*,
<http://www.cbsnews.com/stories/1998/12/03/national/main24233.html>

Mlive.com, *Everything Michigan*, *Seth Privacky: 10 years later – No way to heal*,
<http://blog.mlive.com/news_impact/2008/11/seth_privacky_10_years_later_n/princ/html>

*The Michigan Daily Online*, "Teen Confesses To Gunning Down Family,"
<http://www.pub.umich.edu/daily/1998/dec/12-02-98/news.10.html>

*The Michigan Daily Online*, "911 Tapes Describe Murder,"
<http://www.pub.umich.edu/daily/1998/dec/12-04-98/news.14.html>

*The Wacky World of Murder, Mass Murder Figure Sentenced To Prison*, October 31, 2007.

*The Muskegon Chronicle*, Muskegon, Michigan, November 30, 1998.

*The Muskegon Chronicle*, Muskegon, Michigan, December 1, 2, 3, 4, 5, 1998.

## Detroit's Murderous Purple Gang

<http://info.detnews.com/redesign/history/story/historytemplet.cfm?id=8>

*The Detroit News*, Detroit, Michigan, detnews.com. ""Detroit's Infamous Purple Gang," Paul R. Kavieff, <http://info.detnews.com/redesign/history/story/historytemplet.cfm?id=183>

My Jewish Learning.com, "Bootlegging, Fraud, and Murder By A Gang of Detroit Jews" Rabbi David E. Lipman, <http://www.myjewishlearning.com/history_community/modern/modernsocialgangsters/purplegang.html>

TruTV,, "The Purple Gang," Mark Gibben, <http://www.trutv.com/library/crime/gangsters_outlaws/gang/purple/1.html>

"The Purple Gang," *Wikipedia, The Free Encyclopedia*,
<http://en.wikipedia.org/wiki_purple_gang>

*The Detroit News*, Detroit, Michigan, <detnews.com>. "The Purple Gangs' Bloody Legacy," Susan Whitail

## The Murdering Meat Packer Of Chicago - Adolph Luetgert

*Haunted Chicago, The Sausage Vat Murder, Ghosts and Ghoulish Surrounding A Horrible Historic Murder,* Troy Taylor, 1999, <http://www.prairieghosts.com/sausage.html>

The Birth of Forensic Anthropology, Early forensic science in the United States,
<http://knol.googl.com/k/michel-kelleher/the-birth-of-forensic-anthropology/2x8tp9c7ko.html>

*The New York Times*, New York, New York, July 31, 1899

"This Old Palette: Reflections on the past, present and future of Chicago's palette and chisel academy of fine art. The sausage vat murder trial of Adolph Luetgert," March 3, 2007.
<http://thisold palette.blog.com/2006/09/frank-holme-illustration-murder-trial.html>

# References

"The Sausage Vat Murder Mystery, Patrick Bernauw," 2009, <http://www.unexplained-mysteries.com/viewnews.php?id=148163>

*The Waterloo Courier*, Waterloo, Iowa, September 29, 1897, October 27, 1897.

## Detroit's Most Prolific Serial Killer - Shelly Brooks

*Serial Killer News*, "Serial Killer get another 25 + years," <http://crimezz.net>

Associated Content, "Serial Killer Suspect Shelly Andre Brooks Convicted in Detroit," Jeanne Marie Kerns, March 08, 2007. <http://.www.assiociatedcontent.com>

MyFOXdetroit.com, "Problem Solvers: Mack Avenue Killer Sentenced," March 29, 2007, March 16, 2009, <http://www.myfoxdetroit.com>

## Wisconsin's Original Serial Killer - Eddie Gein

Court TV Crime Library, *Serial Killers: Most Notorious, Eddie Gein*, <http://www.crimelibrary.com>

Ed Gein, *Wikipedia, The Free Encyclopedia*, <http://en.wikipedia.org/wiki/ed_gein>

*Milwaukee Sentinel*, November 19, 20, 21, 22, 1957.

"Dead Men do Tell Tales," *Wisconsin's "Psycho" The Deviant Life And Times Of Ed Gein*, <http://www.prairieghosts.com>

*Oshkosh Daily Northwestern*, Oshkosh, Wisconsin, November 21, 1957.

Plainfield, Wisconsin, *Wikipedia, The Free Encyclopedia*, <http://en.wikipedia.org/wiki/plainfield,_Wisconsin>

*Stevens Point Daily Journal*, Stevens Point, Wisconsin, November 18, 19, 20, 21, 1957.

*Stevens Point Daily Journal*, Stevens Point, Wisconsin, January 23, February 22, 1968.

"Weird Wisconsin," "Wisconsin's Psycho," by Troy Taylor, <http://www.weird-wi.com>

*Wisconsin State Journal*, Madison, Wisconsin, November 18, 19, 20, 21, 1957.

*Wisconsin State Journal*, Madison, Wisconsin, February 11, 1968.

## Michigan's Coed Murderer - John Norman Collins

*The Ann Arbor News*, Ann Arbor, Michigan, August 8, 1967

*The Ann Arbor News*, Ann Arbor, Michigan July 22, 1969.

*The Ann Arbor News*, Ann Arbor, Michigan August 4, 12,15, 16, 18, 19, 20, 1970.

*The Holland Evening Sentinel*, Holland, Michigan, August 2, 1969.

*The News Palladium*, Benton Harbor, Michigan, August 2, 4, 20, November 8, 18, 1969.

*The News Palladium*, Benton Harbor, Michigan, June 3, August 15, 20, 1970.

*The News Palladium*, Benton Harbor, Michigan, October 22, 1977.

*Daily Globe*, Ironwood, Michigan, August 8, 1969.

*Daily Globe*, Ironwood, Michigan, August 19, 1970.

*Traverse City Record Eagle*, Traverse City, Michigan, January 17, 1973.

*Wisconsin State Journal*, Madison, Wisconsin, August 20, 1970.

## The Sick Mind Of Jeffery Dahmer

CourtTV, Crime Library, "Jeff Dahmer, A Notorious Serial Killer And Cannibal," <http://www.crimelibrary.com/serial_killers/nortorious/dahmer>

*Milwaukee Sentinel*, Milwaukee, Wisconsin, July 25, 26, 27, 28, 1991.

*Wisconsin State Journal*, Madison, Wisconsin, July 24, 25, 26, 27, 28, 1991.

*Logansport Pharos-Tribune*, Logansport, Indiana, December 16, 1994.

*Daily Herald, Chicago*, Illinois, August 3, 4, 17, 1991.

*Daily Herald, Chicago*, Illinois, May 17, November 21, 1992, August 3, 1991.

*Daily Herald, Chicago*, Illinois, May 17, August 3, 1991.

# Great Lakes Serial Killers

*Estherville Daily News*, Estherville, Iowa, March 14, April 11, 1992.

*Daily Globe*, Ironwood, Michigan, August 7, 1991, November 30, 1994, November 29, 2004.

*The Logansport Pharos – Tribune*, Logansport, Indiana. December 16, 1994.

## Interstate Murderers - Coleman And Brown

*Wikipedia, The Free Encyclopedia*, Alton Coleman, <http://en.wikipedia.org/wiki/alton_coleman>

The Francis Farmer Revenge Web Portal, Alton Coleman and Debra Brown, <http://www.thefrancisfarmerrevenge.com/stuff/serialkillers/coleman.htm>

*Chicago Tribune*, Chicago, Illinois, June 20, 21 1984

*Chicago Tribune*, Chicago, Illinois, July 20, 21,22 1984

*Detroit News*, Detroit, Michigan, July 12, 13, 30, 31 1984

## All My Best, Belle - Belle Gunness

*Deadmen Do Tell Tales, Belle Gunness: Indiana Serial Killer*, "Come prepared to stay forever," <http://www.prairieghosts.com/belle.html>

*Forest Park Review*, Forest Park, Illinois, May 21, 2008.

Kelleher, C. and Kelleher, Michael, *Murder Most Rare*, Dell, New York, New York, 1998.

La Porte County Historical Society, La Porte, Indiana, <http://www.laportecountyhistory.org/belleg1.html>

*Newark Advocate*, Newark, Ohio, June 18, 1930.

*San Antonio Light*, San Antonio, Texas, July 16, 1946.

*The Legend of Belle Gunness*, La Porte County Public Library, <http://www.alco.org/libraries/lcpl/belle.html>

*The New York Times*, November 27, 1908.

The History of La Porte, Indiana, <http://www.lapcat.org/genelogy.html>

"Belle Gunness; The Black Widow of La Porte" <http://usersites.horrorfind.com/horror/bedlambund/library/gunness.html>

True Crime Library, *Belle Gunness, The notorious Black Widow*, Joseph Geringer, <http://www.trutv.com/library/crime/serial_killers/history/gunness/index_1.html>

## Chicago's Infamous St. Valentine's Day Massacre

*The New York Times*, New York, New York, October 1, 1922.

"The Michigan Whisky Rebellion"' Allen May, Crime Magazine and Encyclopedia of Crime, <http://www.crimemagizine.com/michiganwhiskyrebellion.html>

*The Chicago Tribune*, Chicago, Illinois, February 23, 1920.

*The New York Times*, New York, New York, February 24, 1920

*The Detroit Free Press*, Detroit, Michigan, January 1, 1917.

*The Detroit Free Press*, Detroit, Michigan, April 28, 1918, May 1, 1918.

*The Detroit Free Press*, Detroit, Michigan December 27, 1919. February 19, 21, 22, 1919.

*The Times Herald*, Port Huron, Michigan, February 20, 1919

*The Detroit News*, Detroit, Michigan, April 30, 1918.

Gervais, C.H., "The Rumrunner: a Prohibition Scrapbook," Firefly Books, Thornhill, Ontario, 1980.

## The Intelligent Murderers - Leopold And Loeb

*Crime Magazine; An Encyclopedia Of Crime*, "Leopold and Loeb's Perfect Crime," by Dennis Noe, February 29, 2004.

"Leopold and Loeb," Marianne Rackliffe, <http://www.leopolandloeb.com>

*Wikipedia, The Free Encyclopedia*, Leopold and Loeb, <http://en.wikipedia.org/wiki/leopold_and_loeb>

*Famous American Trials*, "Illinois v.Nathan Leopold and Richard Loeb," <http://www.law.umkc.edu/faculty/projects/trials/leoploeb.html>

Higdon, Hal, Leopold & Loeb: *The Crime of the Century*.

*Homicide in Chicago 1870 – 1930, 1924: Leopold and Loeb*, <http://homicide.Northwestern.edu/crimes/lepold/>

TruTV Crime Library, "Leopold and Loeb," Marilyn Bardsley, <http://www.trutv.com>

## Death By Hanging - William Williams

*Austin Daily Herald*, Austin, Minnesota, April 14, 1905.

*Austin Daily Herald*, Austin, Minnesota, February 13, 1906.

*Logansport Reporter*, Logansport, Indiana, April 14, 1905.

*Star Tribune*, Minneapolis, Minnesota, February 12, 2008.

*The Eau Claire Leader*, Eau Claire, Wisconsin, February 14, 1906.

*The Minneapolis Tribune*, Minneapolis, Minnesota, February 7, 1906.

Trenerry, Walter N., *Murder in Minnesota*, Minnesota Historical Society Press, St. Paul, Minnesota, 1985.

*Waterloo Times-Tribune*, Waterloo, Iowa, April, 13, 1905.

*Wikipedia: The Free Encyclopedia*, William Williams, <http://www.wikipedia.com>

## The Homicidal H. H. Holmes

*Anglo-American Times*, Middlesex, United Kingdom, July 17, 1891.

CourtTV, Crime Library, "H. H. Holmes: Master of Illusion," <http://www.crimelibrary.com/features/fea_serialkiller>

Larson, Erik, *The Devil in White City*, New York, Crown, 2003

*Wikipedia, The Free Encyclopedia*, Dr. Henry Howard Holmes, <http://en.wikipedia.org/wikepedia/H_HHolmes>

*Weird and Haunted Chicago*, "The Murder Castle of H.H. Holmes," <http://www.praieghosts.com/holmes.html>

*Oakland Tribune*, Oakland, California, May 7, 1896

*The Daily Herald*, Chicago, Illinois, February 6, 1993.

*The Mediadrome, American Gothic: The strange life of H. H. Holmes*, Debra Pawlak, <http://www.themediadrome.com/content/articles/history_articles/holmes.html>

*The Postal Card*, Fayette, Iowa, May 5, 1893.

*The Weekly Wisconsin*, Milwaukee, Wisconsin, May 9, 1896

## The Vicious Rapes And Murders Of Paul Bernardo And Karla Homolka

CBC News, <http//www.CBC.ca/news/background/bernardo>, June 25, 2008.

CBC News, <http//www.CBC.ca>, June 10, 2008.

CBC News, <http//www.CBC.ca>, June 7, 2007.

TruTV, <http://wwwtrutv.com>, Paul Bernardo and Karla Homolka, Marilyn Bardsley.

*Wikipedia, The Free Encyclopedia*, Karla Homolka, <http://en.wikipedia.org/wiki/karla_homolka>

*Wikipedia, The Free Encyclopedia*, Paul Bernardo, <http://en.wikipedia.org/wiki/paul_bernardo>

*Newsweek*, "The Barbie and Ken Murders," December 6, 1993, page 36.

*The Homolka Letters*, Stephen Williams, <http://v1.theGlobeandmail.com>

Burnside, Scott, Alan Cains, Deadly Innocence, Warner Books, New York, New York, 1995.

*Winnipeg Free Press*, Winnipeg, Manitoba, Canada, May 1, 1992.

# Great Lakes Serial Killers

*Winnipeg Free Press*, Winnipeg, Manitoba, Canada, May 14, 22, December 19, 1993.

*Winnipeg Free Press*, Winnipeg, Manitoba, Canada, September 24, December 7, 9, 24, 1996.

## The Clown Of Death - John Wayne Gacy

*The Chronicle Telegram*, Elyria. Ohio, January 22, 1979.

*The Chronicle Telegram*, Elyria. Ohio, March 16, 1986.

*The Daily Herald*, Mount Prospect, Illinois, December 29, 1978.

*The Daily Herald*, Mount Prospect, Illinois, December 23, 29, 30, 1979.

*The Daily Herald*, Mount Prospect, Illinois, July 10, 1980.

*The Daily Herald*, Mount Prospect, Illinois, May 12, 1983.

*The Daily Herald*, Mount Prospect, Illinois, February 9, 1992.

*The Daily Herald*, Mount Prospect, Illinois, May 7, 8, 9, 10, 11, 1994.

*European Stars and Stripes*, August 13, 1982.

Court TV's Crime Library, "Criminal Minds and Methods, John Wayne Gacy," <http://www.crimelibrary.com>

## The Murderous Anna Hahn

*Sunday Times Signal*, Zaneville, Ohio, December 6, 1937.

*Evening Independent*, Massillon, Ohio, October 11, 1937.

*The Lima News*, Lima, Ohio, April 5, 1938.

*Mansfield News Journal*, Mansfield, Ohio, April 4, 1938.

*Wikipedia, The Free Encyclopedia*, <http://en.wikipedia.org/wiki/anna_marie_hahn.html>

TruTv, "Arsenic Anna: The true story of Anna Marie Hahn," <http://www.trutv.com/library/crime/notorious_murders/women/anna_hahn/index.html>

## The Sparling Family Is Dying

*Lakeshore Guardian*, Countryside Yarns, The Sparling Murders parts 1 & 2, Janis Stein, February, March, April, May, June, 2008.

*Huron Daily Tribune*, New Novel re-examines 100-year-old murder mysteries, August 29, 2008.

*Huron Daily Tribune*, December 1,15, 22, 1911.

*Huron Daily Tribune*, April 5, 12, 19, 26, 1912.

*Huron Daily Tribune*, May 3, 10, 17, 24, 31, 1912.

*Huron Daily Tribune*, January 5, 12, 19, 26, 1912.

*Huron Daily Tribune*, February 2, 1912.

*Huron Daily Tribune*, June 7, 14, 1912.

*Huron Daily Tribune*, July 12, 1912.

Wrongly convicted database, Dr. Robert MacGregor, <http://forejustice.org/db/location/MacGregor−Dr.-Robert.html>

## From Prophet To Prisoner - Jeffery Lundgren

*The Kirkland Massacre*, by Cynthia Statter Sasse and Peggy Murphy Widder, Kensington Publishing Company, 1992.

*Prophet of Death, The Mormon Blood Atonement Killings*, Pete Early, Replica Books, 1998.

Jeffery Lundgren, OSP # A235-069, State of Ohio Adult Parole Authority, Columbus, Ohio, September 26, 2006.

Jeffery Don Lundgren, <http://www.clarkprosecutor.org>

TrueTv, "The story of Jeffery Don Lundgren, <http://www.trutv.com>

Jeffery Lundgren, <www.rickross.com/groups/lundgren.html>

*USA Today*, October 24, 2006, "Oho excecutes cult leader, Killer of five."

# References

## The Madman of Bath, Michigan - Andrew Kehoe

"Bath School Disaster," *Wikipedia*, <http://www.wikipedia.org>

*Bath Massacre*, Arnie, Bernstein, University of Michigan Press, 2009.

Assortment, "The bombing of the Bath Consolidated Schools" <http://www.essortment.com>

Rootsweb, "The Bath School Disaster" <http://www.freepages.history,rootswebancestry.com>

"The Bath School Disaster," Monty J. Ellsworth, 1927.

*The Mediadrome*, "Just another Sunny Day: The Bath School Disaster" <http://www.themediadrome.com>

*The State Journal*, Lansing, Michigan, May 18, 1927.

TruTv Crime Library, Mark Gado, "Hell Comes to Bath," <http://www.trytv.com>

*The News-Palladium*, Benton Harbor, Michigan, August 11, 1966.

*The Lima News*, Lima, Ohio, May 19, 1927.

*The Ludington Daily News*, Ludington, Michigan, May 18, 1927.

## The Mad Butcher Of Kingsbury Run

"Casebook: Jack the Ripper," Stephen P. Ryder and Johnno, <http://www.casebook.org>

*Cleveland Memory*, Kingsbury Run, <http://www.images.ulib.csuohio.edu>

*Cleveland Torso Murders*, "The Mad Butcher of Kingsbury Run," <http://www.torsomurders.com>

*Chronicle Telegram*, Elyria, Ohio, February 15, 1989.

"Dead Ohio," Kingsbury Run, <http://www.deadohio.com>

*San Antonio Light*, San Antonio, Texas, April 4, 1937.

*The Salt Lake Tribune*, Salt Lake City Utah, October 18, 1936.

TruTv, "The Kingsbury Run Murders or Cleveland Torso Murders," Marilyn Bardsley, <http://www.trutv.com>

The Cleveland Police Museum, Torso Murders, <http://www.clevelandpolicemuseum.org>

*The Daily Courier*, Connellsville, Pennsylvania, July 8, 1939.

The Crime Library, "The Cleveland Torso Murders, Elliot Ness Serial Killer Case," <http://www.crimelibrary.com>

*The Lowell Sun*, Lowell, Massachusetts, July 8, 1939.

## The Serial Killer Of Rochester, New York

"Into the Abyss, The Arthur Shawcross story: Sins of the Flesh," <http://www.members.tripod.com>

*The Democrat and Chronicle Newspaper*, Rochester, New York

"The Democrat and Chronicle.com, Shawcross from 1972- 1990's," <http://www.democratandchronicle.com>

"Serial Killers A-Z, Arthur Shawcross," <http://www.geocities.com>

*Wikipedia, The Free Encyclopedia*. Arthur Shawcross, <http://www.wikipedia.org>

RocWiki; "The peoples guide to Rochester," Arthur John Shawcross, <http://www.rocwiki.org/arthur_shawcross>

TruTv, "The Genesee River Strangler," Katherine Ramsland, <http://www.trutv.com>

*The New York Daily News*, New York, New York, November 11, 2008

## The Monster Of Philadelphia - Gary Heidnik

"New Criminologist: The Online Journal of Criminology, Gary Heidnik and His Cellar of Death," <http://www.newcriminologist.com>

Philadelphia Magazine, "Inside the House of Heidnik," By Victor Fiorillo <http://www.phillymag.com/articles/inside_the_house_of_heidnik/page7>

## Great Lakes Serial Killers

The Frances Farmer Revenge Web Portal; "Serial Killers Live Here, Gary Heidnik," <http://www.francesfarmerrevenge.com>

TruTv.com, "Gary Heidnik: To Hell and Back," Patrict Bellamy, <http://www.trutv.com>

"The Serial Killer Calendar, Gary Heidnik," <http://www.serialkillercalendar.com>

"Dead Silence; the Serial Killer Blog, Gary Heidnik," <http://www.deadsilence.wordpress.com>

"Serial Killer Crime Index, Heidnik, Gary Michael," <http://www.crimezzz.net>

### Killer Without A Conscience - William Heirens

*Alton Telegraph*, Alton, Illinois, August 3, 2007.

*Chicago Tribune*, Chicago, Illinois, April 4, 2002.

*Daily Journal-Gazette*, Mattoon, Illinois, January 8, June 29, 1946.

*Racine Journal Times*, Racine, Wisconsin, January 1, 1946.

*The Daily Register*, Harrisburg, Illinois, December 11, 1945.

The Frances Farmer Revenge Web Portal, "William Heirens: The Lipstick Killer," <http://.www.francesfarmerrevenge.com>

*The News Palladium*, Benton Harbor, Michigan, July 27, 1946.

TruTv, Joseph Geringer, "William Heirens," <http://.www.trutv.com>

# About The Author

Geography has played an important part in shaping Wayne "Skip" Kadar's love of the Great Lakes. Throughout his life he has lived in the downriver area of Detroit, Marquette, Harbor Beach and at the family cottage in Manistique, Michigan. Growing and living in these rich historic maritime areas has instilled in him a love of the Great Lakes and their maritime past.

This love has taken him in many directions. He is a certified S.C.U.B.A. diver and avid boater, having owned most all types of boats from Personal

*Photo by Karen Kadar*

Water Craft to sailboats to a small cruiser. He is involved in lighthouse restoration, serving as the Vice President of the Harbor Beach Lighthouse Preservation Society.

Mr. Kadar enjoys studying and researching Great Lakes maritime history and has made presentations on maritime history on a local, state and international level.

An educator for thirty years, Mr. Kadar retired after 15 years as a high school principal.

In this book, Kadar explores another of his interests: true crime stories. Since attending college during the John Norman Collins murder spree, Skip has followed major crimes occurring around the Great Lakes region.

Skip lives in Harbor Beach, Michigan, with his wife, Karen. During the summer Skip can usually be found at the Harbor Beach Marina, on the family boat "Pirate's Lady" or at the Harbor Beach lighthouse.